SIXTEEN TIMES ROUND CAPE HORN

SIXTEEN TIMES ROUND CAPE HORN:

The Reminiscences of
Captain Isaac Norris Hibberd

With a Foreword by
Frederick H. Hibberd

MYSTIC SEAPORT MUSEUM, INCORPORATED
MYSTIC, CONNECTICUT
1980

Copyright 1980 Mystic Seaport Museum, Inc.
ISBN 0-913372-15-3

FOREWORD

ISAAC NORRIS HIBBERD, MY FATHER, WAS BORN AT DARBY, PENNSYLVANIA, IN 1862. He left his father's farm when about nineteen to go to sea on sailing ships and continued in maritime activities for the rest of his life. He died in 1934 at the age of seventy-two. His eleven years at sea included nine roundings of Cape Horn as a "boy," seaman, and mate, and seven roundings as master, for a total of sixteen. Three voyages were made as master of the *Cyrus Wakefield*, a large, beautiful, and fast ship of which he took command at age twenty-five. In her, he set the speed record for a round trip voyage under sail from San Francisco to Liverpool and return. This record is acknowledged by Frederick C. Matthews in *American Merchant Ships 1850-1900* (Salem, 1920) and Basil Lubbock in *The Down Easters* (Boston, 1929).

The late nineteenth century was the period when steam replaced sail all over the oceans of the world, but trade routes between the west coast of the Americas and the Atlantic ports of North America and Europe were exceptions. Until the opening of the Panama Canal in 1914, sail had an advantage on these routes because of their great length. These trades were dominated by the "Down Easters," large, burdensome but fast square-rigged wooden vessels, most of which were built "down east" in the shipyards of Maine.

Much of Isaac Hibberd's career under sail was spent in vessels built and owned by Samuel Watts (1812-1900) of Thomaston, Maine. Like Hibberd, Watts had gone to sea at age nineteen and became master at twenty-five. He commanded several vessels owned by Edward O'Brien of Thomaston, and retired to join O'Brien as a partner in a general store and shipyard. Striking out on his own in the late 1850s, Watts and his brother built and retained managing ownership in twenty-four ships, one bark, and seventeen schooners, and managed six other vessels. Capt. Hibberd first went to sea in Watts's *Jane Fish*, and rose to master in Watts's renowned *Cyrus Wakefield*, named for a Massachusetts furniture manufacturer. The *Alex. Gibson*, Hibberd's final command, was built and owned by Watts's former employer and partner Edward O'Brien.

The "Down Easters" survived by accepting charters to carry whatever cargo was available. Commonly, coal or high volume, low premium mixed cargoes of bulk and manufactured goods were carried to the West Coast. Grain was loaded at San Francisco for shipment to the East Coast or Europe. In slack times, the vessels carried lumber along the Pacific coast, took South American guano to Europe for fertilizer, or were laid up to await a rise in freight rates. Movement of these vessels was controlled by agents, such as Capt. James Chapman of San Francisco, who gave Capt. Hibberd his first command. With telegraphic communication, the agents kept abreast of available cargoes and world demands, and directed their vessels accordingly. Many times, as on Isaac Hibberd's first passage to Europe in the *Jane Fish*, the shipmaster did not know where his cargo of grain would be delivered until he reached Falmouth, England, or Queenstown, Ireland, and received orders from the vessel's agent. By the 1890s, improved efficiency of the marine steam engine further reduced the employment of the big sailing vessels, and Capt. Hibberd, like many men, sought more secure positions ashore.

After retiring from the sea as a sailing ship master, Capt. Hibberd spent six years as superintendent of the George W. McNear grain warehouses at Port Costa, California. In 1898, he went to Alaska to superintend construction and operation of a fleet of steamers on the Yukon River for the Northern Commercial Co. This was the period of the Klondike Gold Rush, when a steady flow of men and materials was carried by steamer up the Yukon River to Dawson.

Capt. Hibberd spent his later years in and around San Francisco. He served as superintendent of the Pacific Coast Steamship Co.; was a member of Barneson & Hibberd, a shipping firm which also operated piers and warehouses on the San Francisco waterfront; and was active on the Board of Pilot Commissioners for the port of San Francisco.

The ensuing narrative was written by Capt. Hibberd and describes his activities at sea from 1881 to 1892. The portions describing his work as superintendent of the McNear grain warehouses and his activities in Alaska are not included here.

The typescript surfaced recently almost by accident in my file of family papers. I cannot account for why it lay unread for so many years. As my father did not use a typewriter, it must have been dictated or transcribed from a hand-written original; but he signed the first page so he must have seen and approved the typed copy. Internal evidence suggests that it was written (or at least finished) in about 1931. His years at sea and in Alaska were certainly the most strenuous and dramatic and must have appeared to him as the most important of his life. It seems remarkable that anyone with no formal schooling beyond the age of fourteen could express himself so graphically and at times almost philosophically.

Having come upon this picture of a fast disappearing era, I deemed it imperative that it not be lost, and have prevailed upon Mystic Seaport (they were not unwilling) to issue my father's autobiography in print.

What follows should give the reader a picture of a man and a time not to be seen again.

FREDERICK H. HIBBERD

CONTENTS

Foreword	iii
From Farm to Sea	1
A Sailor's Work	2
Off to San Francisco	3
Cape Horn	4
San Francisco	5
To Liverpool via Pitcairn Island	6
Food at Sea	8
Learning to Navigate	9
Atlantic Crossings	10
Shift to Steamers	11
Mate of the *Cyrus Wakefield*	12
Pitcairn Again	14
Liverpool, to New York	15
Another Cape Horn Rounding	16
Sometimes the Crews were "Hard Cases"	18
First Aid at Sea	19
Adrift near Shore	19
New York, to San Francisco	20
Dublin	21
At Sea again with another Captain	23
Do Animals Reason?	23
Man Overboard	24
Sudden Storm	25
Thirty Men Confined for Four Months	26
Master of the *Cyrus Wakefield*	27
To Liverpool and Back	28
Mirages at Sea	30
Record Voyage	31
Along the West Coast	32
A Question of Taste	33
Le Havre	35
The Long Walk	36
Master of the *Alexander Gibson*	36
Stormy Passages	38
Heavy Weather to New York	39
Trouble with the Brooklyn Bridge	40
Last Time Round the Horn	40
A Job Ashore	41
List of Passages Round Cape Horn	43

SIXTEEN TIMES ROUND CAPE HORN

I HAVE OFTEN BEEN ASKED WHAT IT WAS THAT INFLUENCED ME TO TAKE UP life at sea. This was a reasonable question because most of those asking it knew that I was born in a little Quaker settlement outside of Philadelphia, where my forefathers settled in 1680. They had always been farmers and the property is still in the family. No one from my own family, nor any member of the community, had ever shown any sign of caring for the sea. This is the first time that it has ever been answered. It came about in this way.

I had to give up school when I was fourteen years old, as the famous panic of 1873 had about wiped out the financial resources of the family. This made it impossible for me to have the training which would enable me to take up the profession I wanted to — that of medicine.

After the panic, business in Philadelphia was very dull for several years, and there were not many openings for country boys, so I went to work on the farm. As I worked in the corn and hay fields in the hot summer days, I could look across Hog Island and see the vessels passing up and down the Delaware, and I thought how pleasant it must be to sit around on one of those big vessels, with their white sails, and let the wind blow you along with no effort on your part. One particularly hot day, while working with my father, we were looking at a beautiful four-masted schooner sailing majestically up the river towards Philadelphia, and my father made the remark, "to be the captain of a vessel like that would be a gentleman's job." I then and there made up my mind that I was going to have one of those jobs, and commenced to haunt the shipping offices along the waterfront in Philadelphia, going aboard the different vessels lying at the wharves.

One of the first vessels I went aboard after this decision was a small bark called the *Sunbeam*, bound for Portugal. The old captain listened to my story and then he said: "No, I won't take you with me because I'll only be thirty days on the voyage. You'll be sick most of the time and you will not have overcome your dislike of the strange conditions and difficulties of life at sea, and therefore will leave the ship in a foreign country, which will mean a lot of hardship for you. If you want to go to sea, secure a berth on one of the vessels trading between here and San Francisco. This is a four months' trip and you will have plenty of time to get over your seasickness, homesickness, and become accustomed to the work and living conditions, and so find out definitely whether or not you want to follow seafaring for a livelihood, and if, at the end of the voyage, you find you do not care for the life of the sea, you will have landed in your own country and have four months' pay coming to you, which will enable you to take care of yourself until you can get a job on shore."

A Sailor's Work

Well, I did not altogether agree with the old captain's reasoning, but I accepted his advice, and before my first trip was over understood how good and sound it was.

My first voyage was from Philadelphia to San Francisco in 1881, a trip of 136 days, in the ship *Jane Fish*. My wages were $8.00 per month, and when I heard the mate's pay was $50.00 per month, I wondered how he was able to spend it. I have learned that, with some other things, since then.

It is hard to imagine a greater change in conditions than that which would come to a young country boy who had been brought up on a farm from which he had never been twenty miles, than those he found around him when he shipped as a boy before the mast on a ship bound on a voyage around Cape Horn, and whose home life had been that of the ordinary, well-regulated American family. He had had for his playmates and associates those whose connections had lived in the community for over one hundred years. To drop all this and step out into a world consisting of total strangers, living surroundings and working conditions of which he was totally ignorant, was a very different and at first, uncomfortable situation.

And now, what does a green boy do on a sailing ship at first? Generally the things no one else wants to do, such as scrubbing paint, cleaning the decks, taking care of the chickens (if there are any), and generally making himself useful until he shows that he is able to do something better. No one on shipboard ever deliberately tries to teach a boy anything unless he displays a desire to learn, and then he will always find someone to show or tell him what he wants to know. The boy is always expected to go aloft and furl the light sails when they are taken in. These sails are the highest and first to be taken in when the wind freshens. You can imagine it is not a pleasant experience to the seasick greenhorn, on a dark night, to go aloft and furl one of them. This means a climb of one hundred and fifty feet up swaying rigging to a small yard or spar, where he climbs along a rope less than an inch thick, which is the only thing between him and the sea, 150 feet below. As the sail is bellied out with wind, he has to balance himself on the foot rope while he uses both hands to gather in the sail and make it fast to the yard with a small rope called a gasket.

This does not sound inviting, I know, but you soon become used to it and go up on the darkest nights with a gale blowing without ever thinking of there being any danger connected with it. As a matter of fact, I always found it more of a task to go aloft when the vessel was tied up to a dock than I did at sea in a gale of wind.

Captain Gleason Young, master of the vessel, was a fine type of the American seaman, who took care to see that the two green boys were not imposed upon more than was for their good. We were given a little room in the forward house which we shared with the sailmaker. We were not allowed to associate with the sailors except in working hours, being given very strict orders to keep away from the forecastle during our watch below. To us these instructions were not hard to follow, for it seemed to me that the time below was hardly long enough to give us the rest we needed.

In those days the crew was divided into two watches, each being on deck four hours, and then having four hours below. In fine weather when we were running the trades down, it was the custom to keep all hands on deck in their afternoon watch. In other words, the watch that came on deck at eight o'clock in the morning, instead of going below from twelve to four in the afternoon, were given half an hour for dinner and then worked until six o'clock; while the watch that came on deck at twelve o'clock, instead of going below at four o'clock, worked until half-past five, then went below for supper and came on deck at six and relieved the other watch, working until

8:00 p.m. trimming yards and putting the ship in order for the night. This meant that every other day each watch gave up fours hours of the afternoon watch which they were supposed to have below, and one and one-half hours of their dog watch.

So that each watch will not be on deck over the same period each day, it is the custom to divide the hours from four to eight in the afternoon into two watches of two hours each, which are known as the dog watches. Some ships used the system of straight watch and watch (four hours on and four hours off), but most American ships worked on the plan outlined, which was that of the ships I sailed in until I became master.

The American ships were very careful to see that their gear was all overhauled every passage. All blocks were taken down, overhauled, pins scraped and black leaded to be sure there was no question but that they would be in good order when needed. Worn out gear was replaced by new, and all foot ropes, on which the lives of the crew depended when they were aloft furling the sails during heavy weather, were overhauled and care taken to see that they were in perfect condition. The rigging was overhauled and set up; the ship painted fore and aft; every plate and piece of iron and link of chain cleaned and painted; the bright work all cleaned and oiled. Old sails were always bent for use in fine weather and going through the doldrums crossing the equator, and running the trades down. New sails were bent when we approached the Horn, making the land, or any locality where we were likely to experience bad weather. Thus, there was plenty of work to be done. When I first joined the ship, I had an idea that once the ship was washed down and cleaned up she would stay in that condition until she reached the end of the voyage, for I could not see where any dirt could come from out on the ocean. Much to my surprise, I found that this was not the case. The ship needed to be thoroughly washed down at least once a day, and sometimes oftener, and it has always been a marvel to me how so much dirt could collect where apparently there was no opportunity for doing so.

After the *Jane Fish* was loaded, we towed down the Delaware. As soon as we were well clear of Philadelphia, the tugboat came alongside to fill our water tanks. We had one iron tank holding approximately four thousand gallons, which rested on the keelson and reached up to under the upper deck where it was connected by a pump to the main fife rail. There were two wooden tanks on each side of the forward house, holding about one thousand gallons each. During the voyage, whenever it rained, we caught all the water which fell on top of the cabin and the forward house to fill up these spare tanks, and if the rain had lasted long enough to insure that all possible salt and dirt had washed away, the water from the top of the cabin was used to fill up the main tank, so that we always had all the water we needed, provided it was not wasted. That care was exercised is illustrated by the indignant protest of the bosun to the mate, who complained that, "That boy Isaac actually used fresh water to clean his teeth with." This, he seemed to think a criminal waste of good water.

Our first stop after leaving the wharf at Philadelphia was at Wilmington, where we loaded about thirty tons of powder. When I tell you that at the end of the voyage some of the boxes were found to have been broken and the contents loose on the deck, I think you will share my wonderment why it was, in the constant rolling of the ship in bad weather with these heavy boxes shifting over this loose powder which was spread all over the deck, including the iron plates around the hatch, that the ship and any one on board the vessel lived to reach his destination. In fact, there was so much loose powder that when it was taken off out in the Bay of San Francisco before the vessel was allowed to dock, it was cleaned up with large

Off to San Francisco

iron shovels. I have wondered many times what good angel watched over us throughout that voyage when I think how many times those boxes must have moved back and forth over this loose powder.

After leaving Wilmington, we completed our trip down the river and out to the ocean, between Cape May and Cape Henlopen, where we made sail and started on our long voyage around Cape Horn for San Francisco, which port we reached one hundred and thirty-six days later.

While life was rough and hard, it had its compensations, and, judging by my own experience, I think such a trip would be no disadvantage to any normal, healthy American boy. We had it impressed upon us early in our experience that there were two things we must never do. One was not to throw anything overboard to windward, especially hot water and ashes, for if they did not go overboard they would go in our eyes; the other was never to take any food which we had not eaten back to the galley, because if we did the cook might think he was giving us too much and therefore reduce our portion at the next meal. If there was anything left which we did not want to eat (this was very rarely the case, for two growing boys being kept busy in the open air had no trouble in working up a good healthy appetite), we must throw it overboard, being very careful that none of the officers caught us in the act.

Scrubbing paint and cleaning decks did not appeal to me, and I knew if I wanted to get ahead it was necessary to be able to show the mates I had the makings of a real sailor man in me. The bosun was a splendid seaman, but a genuine old growler who, apparently, never had an encouraging word for anyone. I was sure if I could work with him I would soon be able to prove I was more valuable at sailorizing than anything else, especially scrubbing paint. So I used to keep track of what he was doing, and about ten minutes before the bell struck calling the watch on deck, I would slip up to the locker where the bosun kept his gear, and when he came along to put the watch to work, there I was with a tar pot and a grease pot around my neck, and the other tools and supplies he needed (and some he didn't need) hanging on me in various places, so he had nothing to do but growl at me and then tell me to come along with him, which was exactly what I wanted to do.

Cape Horn

Leaving the Atlantic Coast, we had it generally fine down to the equator, where we met with calms, hot and rainy weather. Then more fine weather until we reached Cape Horn, where we found a month of rough weather with heavy winds, snow, sleet, and ice. As the wind there usually blows from southwest to northwest, it was necessary to wear ship frequently in order to take advantage of every opportunity to move westward. Fortunately, we were down there in what was the summer time for that latitude, or at least what they call summer, although to us there was nothing summery about it. It was nothing unusual for us to have to scatter ashes from the galley stove on deck so the men could stand on deck to pull on the ropes when taking in sail. All our clothes would get wet and sometimes we would not be able to have any dry ones for several days, even in bed. Most of the time the vessel was under short canvas, but we finally rounded the corner and started up the Pacific. After leaving the Horn we ran into fine weather, and we had no more heavy gales before reaching San Francisco.

There were many albatrosses flying around us while we were down off the Cape, and whenever the weather permitted we used to take a piece of wire, bend it into a loop, hang a piece of pork in the middle, and trail this over the stern of the vessel. The albatross would come along and snap at the pork. As the upper part of his beak has a sharp hook on the end, all we had to do was pull him in on board, for as long as he resisted with his wings and feet there was no possibility of the loop slipping off his beak, so we were easily able to pull him up on board, and once on board all we had to do was slacken the line and it would drop clear of his mouth. He could have been free any moment had he flown toward the ship instead of trying to pull away from it. These birds have a spread of from six to eight feet in width, and are very graceful while in the air, but they are very awkward indeed when placed on deck and invariably get seasick when they start to walk around on shipboard. It is not necessary to confine them because it is impossible for them to get a start from the deck of the ship, and when you want to let them go, all you have to do is pick them up and throw them overboard. Once in the water, they are perfectly able to take care of themselves because they use their flat feet to gather headway in conjunction with their wings, until they have sufficient speed to allow them to rise up in the air. In fact, their actions in rising from the water are very much like the modern hydroplane, which gathers headway in the water until it has attained sufficient speed to allow it to rise above it.

It is rather difficult to make anyone understand who has not had the experience, how severe the weather is off the Cape. The seas are long and heavy, the weather cold and stormy, and this, combined with the salt water drying on your hands, and the crop of boils which nearly everyone gets, makes the gear hard to handle, because your fingers break open at the joints. It is not unusual to have all of the joints of every finger, on the inside of your hand, crack open down nearly to the joint, so you can imagine it is not very pleasant to have to pull on a cold, wet rope under these conditions, with the sea breaking over the side and ice cold water running down your sleeve. The sails, even when hauled up to the yards ready for furling, are wet and stiff, and with the heavy wind very difficult to gather in so that the gaskets can be passed around them to fasten them securely to the yards. I have been aloft on the topsail yard four hours at a time trying to make the sail fast. Sometimes it was possible to climb up on the yard and then stand up out on the sail, holding on to the lift with your hands in order to press the sail down so that some of the men could get hold of it and haul it up to the yard to make it fast. I remember on one occasion when I reached the deck after such an experience, I found that I had worn the skin off all my fingers and had left bloody marks on the sail where I had been grabbing hold of it in order to pull it up to the yard.

You, who see San Francisco every day, have no idea how good it looked to us after having been one hundred and thirty-six days at sea, and how much we enjoyed the fruit. It seemed to me I had never eaten anything which tasted so good.

San Francisco

My teeth had bothered me a good deal on the voyage, so soon after we arrived I went to a dentist to ask him how much it would cost to put my teeth in order. He said it would take about $60.00. I told him to do $30.00 worth of the most necessary work, and he replied that it was all necessary. I knew it was, but as I only had $40.00 in the world and was three thousand miles from home, and while I was perfectly willing to pay him $30.00 to do the most necessary work, I did want to keep $10.00 for use in emergency.

We stayed in San Francisco about two months and, as there was no one kept by the ship except the mate, carpenter, cook, and myself, I had plenty to do, especially in the cleaning line. Right across the front of the cabin there was a wide strip of copper which it was my duty to keep bright and clean. One day when I was cleaning it, I sat down on the rail scrubbing the copper between my knees, as that was much the easier way to do it. Unfortunately for me, the captain came on board, and from the remarks he made, some of which, properly amplified, were repeated to me, I judged he was not satisfied at such a lazy looking way of doing the work. I then and there made up my mind that thereafter I would never do anything sitting down that it was possible to do standing up.

The old Russian-Finn carpenter was a fine old chap who was always willing to do anything he could for me. I had such a thorough appreciation of his kindness that in later years when I became master of a ship, I made it a point to hunt him up and take him with me. On the first voyage, the carpenter and I would spend many of our evenings in the music halls of the celebrated Barbary Coast, where we used to buy beer and shrimps. We always made a fair division of our purchases, for the carpenter took the beer and I got the shrimps, thus each one of us getting what he wanted.

To Liverpool via Pitcairn Island

We were finally chartered to take wheat to Liverpool and towed to Port Costa to load. When the cargo was on board we came down to San Francisco and anchored in the bay in order to secure a crew. Sailors were very scarce at that time, and it was necessary for every ship to lie in the bay from two to three weeks picking up a crew. While waiting for the crew, the captain bought a supply of chickens, which we kept in a house on the after hatch. As chickens on shipboard have no chance to secure the necessary lime which all fowls require, they almost invariably eat their eggs as soon as they are laid. The only way to overcome this is to give them plenty of oyster shells or similar substances. One day, while we were lying in the bay waiting for the crew, the captain told me to take the small boat, go ashore and get some oyster shells for the chickens. I put three bags in the boat and pulled to shore. After trying in vain to get some oyster shells from the various waterfront restaurants, I was directed to go up to the California Street Market where, they were sure, I could get all I wanted. I had taken three empty sacks with me. I found, upon inquiry at the oyster stand at the market, that they would be very glad to let me have all the shells I wanted. This was over a mile from the boat landing, so there was nothing for me to do but fill up the bags, one at a time, place one on my shoulder, and make three trips down to the landing. When I got back the captain wanted to know why I had been so long over the errand. I explained to him where I had to go for the oyster shells, and that was the nearest place they could be obtained for nothing, and as he had not given me any money and I had none, it was the only way I could get them.

Our crew finally came on board, not much of a crew at that for a full-rigged sailing ship. One old chap had been induced to ship with the understanding that he was to go as the nurse for the captain's sick brother. In fact, when we got to sea, we found there were only three men in the crew who could steer, so, although I only shipped as the boy, it was necessary for me to take my regular trick at the wheel.

We had the usual weather down the Pacific and a fine run through the Northeast Trades, and then a disagreeable time working through the calms, light, baffling airs, and rains of the doldrums, until we picked up the Southeast Trades, which, of course, meant fine pleasant weather. After leaving the trades, we soon picked up the westerlies and headed for Cape Horn. Just before we did this we stopped at Pitcairn Island, a small island about two miles wide by three miles long, approximately 2,000 miles from any other land, made famous by the mutineers of the British sloop of war, *Bounty*, who made it their headquarters after putting all their officers adrift in a small boat in the middle of the Pacific on 24 April 1789.

This is one of the most remarkable trips ever undertaken by a boat of that size. Those of you who are familiar with the comforts provided on the ordinary passenger ship of the present day, can hardly have any conception of the discomforts experienced by nineteen men compelled to live in a boat twenty-three feet in length for a period of fifty days. Too much credit cannot be given Captain Bligh for being able to secure the cooperation of his crew throughout such an experience and finally land safely every one of the men with whom he started out.

After the return of the crew to England, the government made every effort to find out what had become of the mutineers of the *Bounty*. They found that sixteen of them had deserted the *Bounty* at Tahiti, but that nine others had taken the ship and sailed away. Fourteen of the sixteen men were captured and taken back to England and tried by court martial, and three were hanged. Nearly twenty years passed before any further news was obtained of the *Bounty* and the remainder of her crew. In 1808 the captain of an American schooner touched at Pitcairn Island where they found the descendants and one of the original mutineers were still living. After setting their officers adrift, the mutineers had sailed to Tahiti where, having gotten a number of natives, both men and women, on board as visitors, they set sail for Pitcairn. The nine mutineers of the *Bounty* beached the vessel, stripped her of everything which would be of use in building living quarters on the island, then set fire to the hull of the vessel so there would be nothing to attract the attention of passing vessels. They made slaves of the native men and took the women for wives, and their descendants, numbering about 100, were living there at the time of our visit.

The people on the island have no communication with the outside world except through ships making the trip from San Francisco to Europe, most of which sight the island, some stopping for a few hours. We gave them some clothes, medicines, knives, tools, etc., which is all they need, for everything they want to eat grows there in abundance with very little cultivation, so they were glad to give us fruit, chickens, etc., in exchange for what supplies we could let them have.

Ship *Jane Fish*, 1,493 tons, 183.3x38x24, built by Samuel Watts & Co. at Thomaston, Maine, 1868. As she was showing her age, the *Jane Fish* was sold to Norwegian owners in 1882, at the end of Hibberd's passage to England in her. Samuel Watts Collection, Mystic Seaport Museum.

There is no anchorage at the island, the ship being hove to while the natives come off to trade with the passing vessels. The island is about 1,000 feet in elevation. When I found we were going to stop there, I was very anxious to go ashore, so asked the captain if I might be granted that privilege. He spoke to one or two of the islanders who were on board, asking whether or not it would be agreeable to them to have me do so. They inquired about my morals, whether I used profanity, or had any other habits which would be objectionable. At the time of my visit they were strict adherents of the Church of England and held services every day. Captain Young told them that he thought that no one on the island would be contaminated by my visit, and therefore they expressed their entire willingness to have me go in one of the boats which were going for additional provisions. The people closely resemble the natives of Hawaii, although they are somewhat lighter in color. I found them very pleasant and much interested in hearing what I could tell them about the different parts of the world with which I was familiar, and I have always thought that they had achieved an ideal community spirit and an admirable simplicity of living conditions.

The sailors were so fascinated with the attractions of living on the island that at night, about two hours after we left, someone set fire to the spare sails in the sail locker, hoping to destroy the ship so that we would have to leave the vessel in small boats and go back to the island, where they could live without working for the rest of their lives. Upon examination we found that the fire was in the forward end of the sail locker, and owing to the dense smoke and the fact that the locker was full of sails, it was impossible for us to get at the fire. I noticed that the sails had been put in lengthwise, and taking the end of a rope in my hand I crawled through the smoke, drove it through the bight of one of the sails and struggled out with the end. The crew quickly hauled the sail out while I was endeavoring to get the smoke out of my lungs. As soon as the first sail was out, the bosun picked up the end of the rope and went in and did the same thing to another sail. By the time this sail was out I had recovered from the smoke somewhat and was able to repeat the performance for another sail. The rest of the time the bosun and I took turns in going in, weaving the rope through the bight of a sail, and then struggling out into the air with it. In this way we soon had all the sails out and were able to extinguish the fire without much trouble.

We found that someone had taken a half-barrel of pitch, on which they had placed some shavings, and after putting it under the sails set fire to the shavings. It got hot enough to melt a good part of the pitch and burn holes in some of the sails, and would soon have had headway enough to make it impossible for us to put out, I fear, had we not been able to get the sails out of the locker. It was only after a hard fight that we were able to put it out and save the ship. Had they been successful in their attempt, I might be living in Pitcairn today instead of California.

Food at Sea   Soon after leaving Pitcairn we reached the latitude of the strong westerly winds and headed for the long run to Cape Horn. As the winds were strong and almost always fair, it did not take long for us to reach the Cape. One morning when we were off the Cape, running before a heavy gale, the captain, who was on deck at coffee time while I was at the wheel, noticed that no one came aft to relieve me so that I could have my coffee and asked why it was that I had not been relieved. I told him that I did not drink the coffee on shipboard because I did not like it, owing to the fact that it was always sweetened with molasses. He made no comment, but after that the steward always saw that I had sufficient sugar to sweeten my coffee, which, of course, meant a great deal, for it is hard to make a landsman understand what a cup of coffee means to a sailor at five o'clock on a cold, stormy morning.

We rounded the Cape and started up the South Atlantic where we soon ran into fine weather, and before long picked up the Southeast Trades. In running down the trades we were always on the lookout for an opportunity to catch dolphin or bonita, and whenever any of them were in sight, one of the crew went out and sat on the guys of the martingale, using as bait a piece of white rag tied on a large fishhook. If you caught a bonita it was necessary to have someone there with a bag to drop it in as soon as you hauled it up where it could be landed, because the struggles of the fish were short and sharp and very strong, almost giving one the feeling that they were the result of electric shocks. The dolphin, while gamey and requiring skill to handle, does not present anything like the same difficulties that the bonitas do.

If we noticed a shark following the ship, everybody on board was interested in catching it. In this instance we used to use a large hook with about eighteen inches of chain, to which was attached a rope an inch in diameter. For bait we always chose a good solid piece of salt pork. Sailors have a bitter antipathy for sharks and are always eager to catch them whenever an opportunity presents itself. The meat of this fish is white and delicate. Although it tastes very good no ones cares to eat much of it, for there is always the feeling that the shark has, at some time, made a meal off an unlucky sailor. It has always been a puzzle to me why on all the ships that I ever sailed on it was customary to serve fish on Saturday instead of Friday. This meal consisted of boiled fish, boiled potatoes, if we had any, and small pieces of pork boiled out and fried crisp like crutons.

Our food consisted of either salt beef or salt pork, potatoes while they lasted, and hard tack, with three or four slices of soft bread for supper, at which meal we usually had stewed dried apples, gingerbread, and tea. The cook always started to make his tea about two o'clock in the afternoon and it was kept simmering on the stove until supper time at five o'clock. This, too, was sweetened with molasses. The blacker the tea was (and it was generally about the color of ink) the better the sailors liked it, for they judged its strength by its color.

On the return voyage from San Francisco I commenced to study navigation in my spare time, the captain giving me his sights after he was through with them Sunday afternoon. By the time we reached England I could work up dead reckoning and sights for latitude and longitude, so that by the time we landed I was a full-fledged seaman.

Learning to Navigate

One Sunday morning shortly before we reached Falmouth, the watch on deck was engaged in cleaning out the brass work and getting everything in shape for entrance into the harbor. For the purpose of polishing the brass we were using fine sand moistened with ammonia. It is the usual practice to mix the sand for polishing brass with oil, but Mr. Sampson, the mate, thought the ammonia would be more satisfactory. One of the crew was an old Western Ocean packet rat whose nose had been badly mashed up, and like most old sailors, suspicious of any innovation and eager to take any chance to growl whether there was a reason for it or not. He was outspoken in his statements that there was no strength in the ammonia and kept smelling at it without being able to detect any odor or evidence of its penetrating qualities until he finally got it worked around at an angle which allowed the fumes to work up the channels of his broken nose. Once there it was just as difficult for him to get fresh air to clear it out. It is impossible to adequately describe his contortions while the ammonia was in his nostrils. In fact, it was so funny that I laughed outright with so much vigor that the captain came up out of the cabin to see what it was all about, and instructed the mate to see if he could not arrange to have that boy Isaac make less noise when he was working around the cabin.

We went into Falmouth for orders, and after lying in that beautiful harbor for a few days received word that the cargo was to be delivered in Hull, a port on the eastern coast of England. After our arrival there and once the cargo was discharged, the ship was sold to Norwegian interests. There was a Nova Scotia ship named the *Esther Roy* in Hull at the same time we were, whose commander, Captain James O'Brien, was very friendly with Captain Young, the master of the *Jane Fish*. It was arranged between them that I should go as third mate of the *Esther Roy* from Hull to Norfolk, Virginia. We had a good passage across the North Atlantic, not running into any very heavy weather, and in due time reached our destination.

I left the *Esther Roy* at Norfolk and went to my home in Darby, a little town about half way between Philadelphia and Chester. I returned from what, to my neighbors, was a great adventure and created quite a sensation, and I was invited to numerous social gatherings in order that the neighbors could see just what I looked like. In fact, it reached such a point that my father said to me one day that he hoped the next time I came home I would have grown a tail or a pair of horns so they would have some reason for their curiosity. However, I never was able to achieve that feat.

After staying home a few weeks, I commenced to look around for an opportunity to go to sea again. Captain O'Brien of the *Esther Roy* was kind enough to get me a position as a sailor before the mast on the Nova Scotia bark *Linda*, commanded by Captain James Crowe, which was chartered to carry a cargo of oil from Bayonne, New Jersey, to Rotterdam. The trip from the United States to Europe is much shorter and easier to make than the return voyage. As it was summer time, we did not have any heavy weather on the eastern passage, with the exception of one westerly gale.

Steering a ship running before a gale of wind requires more skill and care than with the wind on any other quarter. One night when the gale was at its heaviest, the mate came to me and asked if I thought I could steer the ship, as he had tried every other man in the watch and the captain had chased them all away and there was nobody for him to send there but me. I told him I thought I could. It was night time, but before going to the wheel I took off my coat and went aft in my shirt sleeves to relieve the man who was steering at that time. Steering the ship under those conditions is, to a certain extent, a matter of instinct. You not only have to watch the compass, but to look at the bow of the ship and see how she is going to act before it is recorded by the compass. I had had a good deal of practice in the *Jane Fish* coming around Cape Horn, and it did not take me very long to get the *Linda* on her course. Captain Crowe, who was a very large, athletic individual, standing about six feet three inches and weighing probably 225 pounds, kept looking in the compass all the time as I gradually got the ship steadied on her course, and then planted himself with his back to the companionway and looked over the stern, as he could easily tell by the wake of the ship whether or not I was keeping her straight. Having first satisfied myself that she was on her course, I had no difficulty in keeping her where she belonged the balance of the watch, but I can assure you I had been kept fully occupied in doing do, for I had to meet the change in the ship's head just a few seconds before it occurred and by anticipating the movements of the vessel, it was comparatively easy to keep her on her course and show a straight wake.

In due course we made the English coast and went up the Channel, through the Straits of Dover and up the entrance to the harbor of Rotterdam, or rather to the oil wharf just below the city, where our cargo was discharged. While we were kept fully occupied during the daytime, we had the evenings to ourselves, and it was very interesting to see the many strange costumes and customs of the new port. After our cargo was discharged, we took on ballast and came back to New York. The passage to the westward was much longer, and as the wind was ahead most of the time, we felt its strength much more than we did running before it going to the eastward.

I left the *Linda* in New York and returned home for a visit. The family objected to my going so far away. In those days, anyone who made a visit to a point fifty miles from home was considered to have made quite a journey, as it usually took four days for the trip there and back. When you think that the same trip can be made today with an ordinary automobile within three hours or less, it shows what a change has taken place. In accordance with the family's wishes, the next time I went to sea I chose one of the fruit steamers of the Warner & Merritt fleet running between Philadelphia and Jamaica. This was a voyage of about a month, and as it was always pleasant weather after we crossed the Gulf Stream, there was very little exposure and hardship connected with this trade. The worst fault that I found with it was the fact that there were only four men in the crew and it was necessary in the daytime for each of us to stand four hour watches at the wheel. While the work, of course, was not heavy, I did not fancy standing in one place for four hours at a stretch. There were many interesting sights to be seen in Jamaica, and I certainly enjoyed having all the bananas, pineapples, and other tropical fruits I wanted to eat. There was not very much about this trade which was attractive to anyone who wanted to become a thorough seaman. Practically all that was required of us was to steer and keep the ship clean. After a few months this became very monotonous and I decided to make a change.

At this time steamers were gradually forcing the sailing ships out of the various trades except the very long ones, such as that between New York and San Francisco around Cape Horn. In those trades, a sailing ship would carry cargo at rates which, while giving the sailing vessel a fair return, were lower than a steamer could possibly hope to meet, for at that time there was no Panama Canal, although the French were doing their utmost to provide one. Some connections of my family were interested in the American Line, which consisted of four large steamers, *Pennsylvania*, *Ohio*, *Indiana*, and *Illinois*, running between Philadelphia and Liverpool. It was pointed out to me that if I would join this company there was every likelihood such ability as I might have would be recognized, and I could look forward to advancement to a good position in the line, and in addition, I would have four or five days home every month. I accepted the suggestion and made an application for a fourth mate's position and was assigned to the *Illinois*, commanded by Captain Warrington.

I joined the ship late in the fall so I had a chance to see what the weather during the winter months in the North Atlantic was really like. It was early impressed upon me that there was much more formality aboard the steamer than on ships I had previously been sailing on. On sailing days we were all dressed up in our uniforms with white gloves, and stationed at our posts while the ship was leaving the wharf. It was one of the rules of Captain Warrington that nobody, under any circumstances, no matter how cold the weather was, should put his hands in his overcoat pockets. We were supposed to wear gloves and fold them behind us as we walked up and down the bridge.

One time when I was on the lookout on the forecastle head going up the Delaware River, cutting through about two inches of ice, and as the wind was ahead, this ice was thrown right into my face as I stood looking forward. It was very cold and in order to keep warm I started to walk back and forth across the forecastle with my hands folded behind my back. I had not been

Shift to Steamers

doing this but a few minutes before the quartermaster came forward with instructions from the captain to me to stand in one place when I was on the lookout. There was, of course, no way of avoiding standing still facing the cold wind, but I did break the rule enough to lift first one foot and then the other in order to increase the circulation. I am happy to say that while I am sure the captain did not approve of this action, he did not send instructions for me to discontinue.

American Steamship Company Philadelphia to Liverpool liner ***Illinois***, 3,104 tons, 357x43x32, 1,800 horsepower compound engine, built by W. Cramp & Sons at Philadelphia, 1873. *Nautical Gazette* Supplement, 3 January 1874.

Mate of the *Cyrus Wakefield*

Shortly before I joined the *Illinois*, during a heavy storm which swept over the bridge of the *Pennsylvania*, the captain and two officers were washed overboard. As a result of this experience, orders were given that at any time the weather was rough all weather cloths on the bridge should be removed. You can imagine what it felt like to be up on one of those exposed bridges way above the water, with the steamer going full speed in a biting wind or snowstorm coming from right ahead. I have often wondered what the officers of the modern steamer, with their almost completely enclosed bridges, would say if they were told that all of this protection would be taken away from them whenever the ship encountered rough weather.

Life on the *Illinois* was interesting and I gained much experience and a thorough knowledge of navigation because the officers had more time to devote to such work than those of the sailing ship, although I must confess that I never could see that they were any more accurate in their work, although they made many more computations than were thought necessary in the sailing vessel.

On my arrival in Philadelphia at the end of a voyage to Liverpool and back, I found a note from Captain Gleason Young, who had been master of the *Jane Fish*, asking me to go as third mate with him on the *Cyrus Wakefield*, a new ship that had made only one voyage, and of which he had been appointed master. The *Wakefield* was a three-skysail-yard ship of over 2,000 tons burden, a very fine example of the best type of ships turned out by Maine shipbuilders. The following quotation which is taken from Basil Lubbock's *Down Easters* gives a good description of the vessel:

"The *Cyrus Wakefield* was the first Thomaston ship to have double topgallant yards, and with her main skysail she had a more lofty and imposing appearance than the other vessels built at that port. She was considered to be the fastest ship ever turned out by Thomaston."

I declined Captain Young's offer saying that I had made up my mind to stay in the steamers. He asked me if I would not at least come to New York and see the *Wakefield*. This I was glad to agree to do, because a fine ship always had a strong appeal to me. After we had looked the ship over together, the captain repeated his offer, saying that if I would go third mate that voyage he would agree to turn her over to me as master at the end of two years. That, of course, seemed to me to be an impossibility and I still held to my intention of staying with the steamers. When I was leaving, Captain Young said to me, "You go home and tell your friends just what I have said to you." This I did and was advised to see Mr. Frank Neal, the vice-president of the American Line.

After listening to my story, Mr. Neal said, "What chances of promotion have you where you are now?" I told him I thought he knew more about that than I did. After thinking a while, he said, "If all things had been equal about you, I would rather you had had a little more experience in sail. Accept his offer and go with him for a year and when you come back you will find you have not lost any time." So I wrote Captain Young that I would accept his offer, and reported for duty on the *Wakefield* [March, 1884].

Soon after I joined this ship a cousin of mine who lived in New York came down to look at the vessel, and when he saw my quarters he was very indignant that I should have to share such a small room with the second mate while the captain had so many rooms for his sole use. I assured him that my quarters were as good as the third mate could expect on any ship of that class. The interesting part about this story is that when I came back to New York about three years later as master of the *Wakefield* and then had all of the captain's quarters for my own use, although my cousin was on board many times, I never heard him express any sympathy for the third mate who was occupying the quarters which I originally had.

The *Wakefield* was chartered to carry general merchandise from New York to San Francisco, and had the usual dispatch in loading her cargo, and after this was on board and the crew shipped, towed out past Sandy Hook and started on her long voyage of 13,000 miles. Our cargo was made up of every variety of merchandise, as it could be carried by ship at a much lower rate than the railroads were willing to accept in those days. We had a large consignment of whiskey which had been shipped in from the Kentucky distilleries. The principal reason for shipping this class of merchandise by sailing ship was that a four months' trip around Cape Horn, where the rolling of the ship kept the whiskey in constant motion, aged it more than four years would if kept in a warehouse on shore. This was also true of California wine which was shipped by sailing vessel around to New York and other eastern ports.

We had the usual run of weather after leaving New York, consisting of variable winds until we struck the Northeast Trades which carried us down to the doldrums, where we spent about ten days working through light baffling airs and calms with much rain until we were able to pick up the Southeast Trades, which carried us down to about 25 degrees south latitude. From there we had variable winds, gradually growing stronger as we approached the Cape, where we ran into the usual heavy weather.

The second mate was laid up off the Cape, so that it was necessary for me to stand his watch, which I did until we were well around into fine weather in the Pacific, when he recovered sufficiently to return to duty. You can imagine that it was no light responsibility for anyone of no more experience than I to have full charge of a big ship like the *Wakefield* in the heavy weather off the Cape. I am quite sure the captain spent more time on deck than he would have done had the second mate been able to take charge of the watch. Nevertheless, the responsibility was mine. Fortunately we met with no accidents and gradually worked to the westward and then up the Pacific until we struck the Southeast Trades which, of course, meant fine weather, giving us an opportunity to overhaul the gear and repair all damage occasioned by the heavy weather off the Cape.

We had our usual experience passing through the doldrums where we had the calms, light airs, and rain which one always experiences in those latitudes. The *Wakefield*, however, was much better fitted to cope with such a situation than the average ship because she was very lofty. It was 173 feet from the deck to her main truck, and I have often seen her skysails full, which gave her steerageway, while the lower sails were hanging limp with no pulling power whatever, a great help in working through the calms and light airs of the doldrums. After working through them, we picked up the Northeast Trades which carried us up to about 25 degrees north latitude. We were then well to the westward of San Francisco, but as the winds in that part of the ocean are generally from the westward, we made a fine run to San Francisco where we discharged the cargo, including the whiskey taken on in New York, all in good condition. We also discharged some of the stone which was used in the construction of the Club Mansion, now the home of the Pacific Union Club. For our return voyage we were chartered to take a cargo of wheat from San Francisco to Liverpool.

As Captain Young and the mate did not work in harmony, the latter decided to leave, and the captain decided to promote me to the position of first mate. This was rather rapid advancement for a man who had no more experience than I, and I was somewhat doubtful about accepting the position, but the captain insisted that I do so, so there was nothing left for me to do but obey instructions, and the result seemed to justify Captain Young's judgment.

Pitcairn Again

We had the usual run down the North Pacific, and after leaving the Southeast Trades we were close to Pitcairn Island where I had previously stopped on my voyage in the *Jane Fish*. As we reached there about noon, Captain Young put the ship aback and waited for the natives to come off, which they did, with some fruit. As Mrs. Young and her little daughter were aboard, the captain was anxious to get a good supply of fresh fruit and vegetables and so arranged with the natives for another boatload. This gave me another chance to go ashore. As I had established a satisfactory reputation on my first trip, there was no difficulty in arranging for my visit, where I renewed the friendships formed on my first voyage.

We spent the afternoon lying off and close to the island, and after the second boatload of fruit was safely on board and our visitors had left with their supplies, we started for our run around the Horn. Having in mind our previous experience off Pitcairn Island, Captain Young and I were on the alert to see that nothing of the kind occurred. I do not know that there was anybody who would have wanted to take the chance, but if there were, they certainly had no opportunity to do so because I saw that everybody on board was kept busy until we were so far away from the island that there was no possibility of anyone wanting to make the trip back there in a small boat.

We had the usual run around the Cape, which, as I said before, is very much easier when you are bound to the eastward. In fact, there is just about the same difference as there is between sliding down an eastern hillside covered with snow in the winter time, and in walking up the same hill pulling the girl on your sled. I do not believe there is a more magnificent sight to be seen anywhere in the world than to be on deck of a full-rigged sailing ship running under topsails before a heavy westerly gale off Cape Horn on a bright moonlight night. You have the Southern Cross and all the stars seem to have a brilliance which is never seen anywhere else. It is impossible to imagine a more magnificent spectacle or one which gives a greater thrill.

After rounding the Horn, we headed up the South Atlantic, having the usual weather until we struck the Southeast Trades, which carried us up to the doldrums where we lost them. We had the usual experience across this strip of water until we found the Northeast Trades at the northern edge, then more fine weather until we got up into the region of regular North Atlantic weather with its prevailing westerly winds. We made Cape Clear, the southern point of Ireland, and then headed up through the Irish Sea for Liverpool, and off Holyhead picked up the towboat which towed us safely into the Mersey.

All ships entering Liverpool are required to rig in their jibboom and put their anchors on the forecastle before they are allowed to dock. We discharged our cargo there and loaded ballast for New York. We had a very stormy passage across. In fact, on the whole trip of forty days there was no twenty-four hours in which I had more than four hours sleep, and at no time did I have this in more than two hours, because it was necessary to make and take in sail and wear ship so frequently that I was able to get very little rest. I dared not stand still a moment when I was on watch for fear of going to sleep, and in fact did go to sleep on one or two occasions when I was walking, and the first thing I knew bumped into the wheelhouse which thoroughly wakened me and banished all thought of sleep for a while.

Liverpool, to New York

We finally reached New York safely and discharged the cargo of salt which we had taken on for ballast. While it was necessary for us to have some cargo on the ship, freight rate on the salt was so low that it barely paid for taking it in and putting it out. Therefore, we did not carry any more than was absolutely necessary since we did not want to lose the time in loading and discharging freight for which we received no revenue.

The question has often been asked me how it was possible for men to go aloft in stormy weather at sea. Strange as it may seem, it is easier to do this than it is to go up aloft in a ship when she is perfectly still, tied up to the wharf. You can understand how this may be true when the ship is laying over with the wind on the beam, but even though this is not the case and she may be rolling from side to side, it is still a fact that it is easier to go aloft under these circumstances than it is when she is safely moored alongside the wharf. This may seem strange, and I have no explanation to offer, but it is undeniably a fact.

On our arrival we found the ship was chartered to load general merchandise to San Francisco in the Sutton & Beebe Line. This cargo was made up of all different sorts of merchandise, care being taken to see that we had some heavy freight in order to bring the ship down to her load line. The freight rate was fixed on the basis of weight or measurement, whichever was most profitable for the ship. This means that the ship had the right to base a charge either on 2,000 pounds weight or forty cubic feet measurement. Pig iron will average about twelve feet to 2,000 pounds, while classes of furniture, dry goods, etc., may measure four times that much before you have 2,000 pounds of weight. For that reason it is clearly understandable why it was to the profit of the ship to have the cargo made up of merchandise, some of which weighed much more than it measured, and other classes of freight which measured much more than it weighed.

Another Cape Horn Rounding

We were about a month in port loading the cargo and then started on our way for San Francisco. We had fine weather down the North Atlantic until we picked up the Northeast Trades, which, of course, meant ideal sailing conditions, for the wind was steady, the weather warm and pleasant. We saw many schools of flying fish, which are very beautiful little creatures who rise up out of the sea like a flock of small birds in their endeavor to get away from the bonita and other large fish which prey upon them. Their flight is generally about 300 feet before they go down into water again. Old sailors have the belief that they can fly as long as their wings are wet. Occasionally one would fly aboard the ship, especially at night, and whoever was lucky enough to find it would take it to the galley and have it cooked for his breakfast. The meat is very delicate, somewhat like that of the trout.

After losing the trades we ran into the doldrums and experienced the usual hot weather, rain, light airs, and calms until we finally worked across the comparatively narrow stretch of such weather and were able to pick up the Southeast Trades. The weather was very pleasant until we approached the River Plate (La Plata), where it is necessary to be on the lookout for very heavy squalls which are occasionally met in that latitude. As we worked farther south toward the Horn, the weather gradually became colder and stormier. One night one of the sailors, who was up in the fore topgallant crosstrees furling the main royal staysail, fell down on deck and was killed. On picking up the body we found that he had on a heavy coat, seven shirts, two suits of underwear, and three pair of pants — hardly the proper outfit for a man to have on when he was climbing up the rigging on a dark night where his actions were guided more by feeling than sight.

We had the usual heavy weather off the Cape, wearing wet clothes nearly all of the three weeks we were in that locality. This meant sore hands, boils, and much general discomfort, but everyone who undertakes a passage to the westward around Cape Horn expects to go through that experience. We were very glad indeed when it became possible to leave this disagreeable weather behind us and work up to the northward in the South Pacific, because of the improved living conditions and added comfort in every way.

As soon as we picked up the Southeast Trades we unbent the new sails we had been using in the heavy weather off the Cape, and bent our old fair weather canvas, overhauled the gear, cleaned the iron work, set up the rigging, and commenced to put the ship in fine shape before we reached port. All of the work preparatory to painting and a final cleaning up of the ship was done in the Southeast Trades because we had fine weather. The winds were steady and everybody could give his attention to the work in hand, for the sails required very little attention. This continued until we reached the doldrums where we met the usual conditions to be found in those latitudes. After working through the doldrums we picked up the Northeast Trades where we completed the work of overhauling the gear and gave the ship, including the yards and masts, a full coat of paint throughout.

One afternoon while we were passing through the trades, I noticed one of the sailors who had been sent aloft to scrape the fore pole seemed to have some difficulty in climbing up there. The pole is that portion of the mast which rises above the rigging. Looked at from the deck it seems to be only about four feet high, but in reality it is generally about eight. After watching the sailor for a few minutes, I thought I would go up and see what was the matter. When I got up to the skysail yard where he was standing, I asked him what the trouble was. He told me he didn't know, but he just couldn't climb that pole. When you realize that the pole was 165 feet from the deck, with the ship rolling from side to side, it is not difficult to understand that it would not be an easy task for anyone not accustomed to such work. I borrowed the man's knife, climbed up the pole and scraped it down to where he could stand on the skysail yard and finish the work. When I reached the deck, Captain Young asked me what I was doing up aloft. I told him just looking around to see if everything was all right. He said, "No, you weren't. You were up there scraping the fore pole." I told him I scraped it while I was up there, and he wanted to know why the sailor who was sent up to do the work hadn't done it. I told him he simply couldn't get up there, I didn't know why because I knew he had been in similar places before, but it was just one of the times when he couldn't possibly make it.

We had fine weather into port, where all the crew, except the carpenter, cook, and myself were paid off just as soon as the ship was docked, the work of discharging the vessel being done by stevedores from shore who were hired for that purpose. We turned out a very satisfactory cargo; in fact, as long as I was in the *Wakefield* I do not believe any insurance company ever paid a dollar's worth of claims, either against the ship or the cargo she carried.

One of my duties that trip was to act as child nurse for the captain's little daughter, for whenever his wife left the ship to go uptown on a shopping expedition, leaving him in charge of a little four-year-old, hardly before she was well clear of the wharf, the captain always had some good reason why it was necessary for him to go up to the office, and therefore it fell to me to look out for the little youngster. We were very good friends and therefore this was no trouble to me, for she would trot around the decks after me whenever I had to oversee some of the work being done.

An old steward came to me to report a conversation between the captain's wife and one of her young lady friends, which he had overheard while he was doing his work around the cabin. It seems that I was the subject

Painting of the *Cyrus Wakefield*, artist unknown. Now in the living room of his son, it was rescued from the Hibberd home in San Francisco during the earthquake and fire of April 1906 by Capt. Hibberd, who cut it from its frame, rolled it up, and put it in his son's baby carriage along with other valuables which were then rushed to safety. In possession of the author.

for discussion. The captain's wife told the young lady that I was a very nice young man, that I did not drink, did not smoke or swear, but she did not know whether I had any other bad habits or not. I have always considered her as a very prudent lady who was willing only to guarantee the subject as far as she knew.

"Hard Cases"

Soon after leaving New York on our way out, one of the sailors came to me and said he was sick. On examining him I found that it was an old trouble which he had acquired many months before joining the ship. He was in such bad shape that he was practically useless throughout the trip, not able to go aloft or do any of the heavy work, being kept at such simple work as checking gear, cleaning paint pots, and doing other chores around the deck. Two weeks after the crew was discharged, I was surprised by a visit from a United States marshal telling me I was under arrest for cruel and inhuman punishment to one of the sailors. Upon inquiring his name, I learned that it was the sick man who had made this charge. As he had never been punished at all; in fact I had given up part of my watch below every day in order to see that he had proper medical treatment, I was utterly at a loss to account for the charge.

I accompanied the marshal to the office and arranged for the necessary bail. The next day I received a letter from an attorney stating that if I would pay $100.00 the case would be dismissed. This I was not willing to do and insisted upon the case going to trial. I had no lawyer and no witnesses. The prosecution had a number of witnesses, but before half of them had given their testimony the judge turned to the United States marshal and asked him if he thought he wanted to go any further with the case. He said no, he was entirely satisfied, and that ended the case.

On my way out I passed the sailor who had brought the charge, and I said to him, "You hadn't much of a case this time, but if you ever sail with me again I think you will likely have a better foundation for a suit when we reach port."

There are many stories of cruel treatment of sailors by their officers, and there were, no doubt, some cases in which this was true, but you must take into consideration the type of hard cases who made up the majority of the crews of the ships in those days. I cannot give a better illustration than to tell of how the crew of one ship, of which I knew the captain very well, was made up.

About thirty-five years ago [1895] in Australia, a number of men were murdered on their way out into the country to look at a prospective gold mine. After a number of cases in which men had not returned from such trips, the authorities' attention was called to the situation. They finally decided that the crimes had been committed by a man named Butler who, they found, had taken these men out into the country on the pretext of showing them a prospective gold mine. All trace of Butler was lost for some time, but the authorities eventually traced his movements so that they were sure he had shipped as a sailor on the *Swanhilda* which had sailed for San Francisco. They communicated with the police in San Francisco and when the *Swanhilda* anchored in the stream, the police boat went out alongside with half a dozen fully armed police officers and found their man, who was eventually extradited to Australia, where he paid with his life for the crimes he had committed.

I asked the captain of the *Swanhilda* if he had had any trouble with the murderer when he was a sailor on board the ship, and he replied that there were a number of men there who were much harder to handle than Butler. In all my experience at sea I have never known an officer to resort to violence unless he was forced to. In fact, the average sailor who knew his business and did his work, received more consideration than some members of various labor gangs working in the woods and in general construction work. You can readily understand that when men of this type are caged up in one small vessel for over four months' time, that there is bound to be more or less dissatisfaction and disagreement among themselves. This is mentioned simply to show that, after all, many of the charges of cruelty brought against mates of vessels had very little foundation.

In due course the ship was chartered to load a cargo of wheat for Liverpool. We had the usual weather down through the North Pacific, across the doldrums and into the Southeast Trades. One night about eight o'clock, while we were running down through the trades, my little charge, the captain's daughter, and the dog were playing down on the main deck. The child slipped and fell, striking her head on a heavy iron ringbolt, and as a result was taken with a severe case of convulsions. The captain came to me and asked me to get some hot water as quickly as possible. As the fire was out in the galley, I knew it would take us some time to get hot water in that manner. It occurred to me that we could get the hot water very quickly by adopting the practice I had seen used when I was a boy on the farm, which was heating stones in a bonfire and then dropping them into the water.

First Aid at Sea

We had a forge in the carpenter's shop and it was the work of only a few minutes to get that out and start it going so we could heat bolts and heavy pieces of iron. As soon as they were hot we took them to the cabin and put them in the water which had already been placed in the bathtub, to which had been added a small quantity of mustard, so that in a very short time we had all the warm water we needed. Of course, in the meantime we had built a fire in the galley so as to insure having all the hot water we could possibly need. It was necessary for me to hold the poor little youngster in my arms in that tub for two hours before we could stop the convulsions, while her father gave her frequent doses of weak solutions of aromatic spirits of ammonia.

We had the usual weather around the Cape, but as the winds were from the westward, giving us a fair wind, we made a quick trip around and were soon up in the pleasant weather of the South Atlantic and commenced our regular program of getting the ship in good condition before we reached Liverpool. After discharging our cargo here we went across to New York. As it was summertime we had fine weather most of the trip, although the winds were generally from the westward. In fact, the heaviest blow that we had struck us a few hours after leaving port, while we were in tow of one of the big ocean tugs.

The wind had been from the south and suddenly changed into the northwest. The tugboat started to haul the ship up to windward, but before he could make much headway the hawser carried away and by the time we could get enough headsail on her to head her off shore, we were almost in the breakers. In fact, I never saw a crew sober up more quickly than ours did that night. Some of the men, who were so drunk that they seemed barely able to navigate, were able to step around very lively when they saw those breakers right close ahead. Fortunately we were able to wear around and go on the other tack, which took us out of danger, and once clear, all our troubles were over, as we had plenty of room in the Irish Sea for maneuvering.

Adrift near Shore

Mrs. Young was very much disgusted the next morning while the captain and I were discussing the incident at breakfast, for all during the years that she had been at sea she had made it a practice to sleep fully dressed whenever there was any sign of rough weather; but this night, the only time there had been any real danger in all the years that she had been with us, she had undressed and gone to bed with a perfect feeling of security because we had a towboat ahead of us to keep us out of trouble. When she realized how serious the danger had been and thought of how unprepared she would have been to meet the situation had the ship actually gone ashore, she was very much annoyed.

This gale was the only real bad weather we experienced on the trip across to New York, for while the winds were generally ahead and our progress slow, we encountered no rough weather and therefore were able to have the ship in fine condition when she reached port. This was a matter of satisfaction to me, for each mate always took much pride in seeing that his particular ship was in fine condition for inspection by the various people who came down to look at her after she was made fast to the wharf. These visitors were familiar with conditions on shipboard and knew whether or not a ship had been properly taken care of, and were not at all backward in expressing their opinion. When you realize that this was the situation in every port, it is easy to understand how much the reputation of the different mates depended upon the reports of these unofficial experts.

New York, to San Francisco

About twenty-four hours before we reached New York, while the weather was beautifully clear, we saw a picture right ahead of us which was an exact duplicate of the harbor of New York with all the principal buildings, both around the waterfront and throughout the entire city. There was a reality about the picture of the city which, if we had not known definitely was 200 miles away, would have given us the impression that we were going to enter the harbor within a few hours. It was a magnificent sight which lasted for about an hour and then slowly disappeared until there was not a trace of it left.

At this time there was a very fierce competition between the pilot boats of New York and New Jersey, and it was not uncommon for us to pick up a pilot 500 miles off shore. These were very welcome visitors, for while they were of no practical use to us until we reached the entrance to the port, they always brought us the latest papers and general news of what was happening in New York. However, we did not pick up our pilot this time until we were within a few hours sail of the port, and soon afterwards we took one of the large ocean tugboats which towed us into anchorage, and as soon as we were through with the customs and quarantine officials, went to our dock on the East River, as we had been chartered to load a general cargo of merchandise for San Francisco.

It was a very impressive sight in those days to walk along South Street and see the jibbooms of these large sailing vessels reaching out over the street almost to the buildings on the opposite side. It was necessary for us to trip up the martingale so that it would not interfere with trucks passing close to the edge of the dock, especially as the ship gradually went down in the water due to the amount of cargo she had taken on board.

Our cargo consisted of the usual merchandise, and in it could be found anything from a paper of pins to a barrel of whiskey, or iron rails to an anchor. By the time the ship was loaded, all the sails had been bent by riggers from shore hired for that purpose, so that there was nothing for the crew to do but take the ship away from the dock and make fast the towline of the tug which was to take us out to sea. Leaving New York going out to sea, we passed down by Governor's Island and the Statue of Liberty, until we were well clear of the land. Here the pilot left us and we commenced to make sail. As soon as we had sufficient canvas set, the towline was cast off and we started on our long trip of 12,000 miles, which we hoped to do in not more than four months.

We landed in San Francisco 133 days from New York. The cargo was discharged and the ship chartered to carry a cargo of wheat to Dublin. As soon as the inward cargo had been taken out, the ship was lined for our wheat cargo. This lining, which usually consisted of about 30,000 feet of lumber, depending on the size of the vessel, is a complete skin for the ship. It is put in in every case where a wooden ship carries a cargo of wheat or barley, which are the only two grains shipped from California in such quantities. This, in turn, is covered with burlap to protect the grain from damage and to insure that if any of the sacks are broken the grain has no chance to work down into the bilges and so interfere with the work of the pumps. As soon as the liners had finished their work, we towed to Port Costa where the cargo was waiting for us, and about two weeks later came down to San Francisco and anchored in the bay to take on our list consignment of stores and be ready for the new crew. This crew proved to be the usual mixture of good, bad, and indifferent sailors, but fortunately there were enough good ones to balance those who were not competent seamen.

We left San Francisco in the evening in company with the ship *Reuce*, a vessel of approximately the same size and bound for the same port. The tugboat towed us out over the bar, where the pilot left us, and as soon as we had sufficient canvas on her to give the ship headway, we cast off the towline and started on our 13,000 mile voyage to Dublin. The ships were less than half a mile apart when night fell, but in the morning we did not see anything of the *Reuce*, nor did we catch sight of her all during our voyage. One hundred thirteen days later, just as day was breaking, I looked around to see if there were any vessels near us, and there, less than a quarter of a mile away, was the *Reuce*. Later the captain of the *Reuce* and I compared log books and discovered that at no time were we more than 200 miles apart.

It seems almost unbelievable that two ships should leave the same port at the same time, and sail for 113 days over practically the same course, bound for the same port, at no time being more than 200 miles apart, and yet never near enough to see each other.

After an uneventful voyage we arrived in Dublin. The characters of Dublin's waterfront have the reputation of being the cleverest people in the world at appropriating for their own use something which belongs to the other fellow. We had an interesting illustration of that. One day about eleven o'clock the steward came running aft to the cabin and told Captain Young somebody had sneaked into the galley while he was setting the table for dinner and stolen the dinner. The captain told him to go back and prepare another one, and when he reached the galley he found that some one else had dropped in and stolen the dishes, which episode was promptly reported to the captain, who told the steward to go to the galley and stay there or the next time they would probably take the stove. But I think the crowning piece of effrontery was when they stole the boots off the night watchman's feet while he was quietly sleeping in the forecastle in the day time in order to be in shape to carry on his duties at night. This happened nearly fifty years ago but I can still remember the indignation of that watchman, and what a fluent description he gave of his opinion of the guilty parties.

These gentry are very clever. It was never safe to lay a block or a piece of rope on the quay and turn your head for a quarter of a second, because, if you did, when you turned it back again neither the block nor the rope would be there. From my experience with them, I am quite sure their reputation is a well-earned one.

Dublin was a very attractive city in those days, especially to one who had never been in Ireland before. Fortunately for me, I became very good friends with all of the stevedores and customs officials so that my experience there was a very pleasant one. I noticed one thing, I had never heard as good English spoken in any part of either England or America as I heard used by

Dublin

the cultivated people of Dublin. As it was summertime the weather was very pleasant and I had many enjoyable short trips to the nearby country.

Ship *Cyrus Wakefield*, 2,013 tons, 247x43.7x28.6, built by Samuel Watts & Co. at Thomaston, Maine, 1882. 10½"x17½" tinted photograph. On the back of a postcard-size photograph of this view Capt. Hibberd noted, "This photograph was taken in the Irish Sea Oct. 29th [sic] 1887 from the deck of the tug which towed us out of the Liverpool docks at the beginning of the last half of what proved to be the record voyage from San Francisco to Europe and return. We were eight months and two days making the 2,600 mile voyage twenty nine days of which were spent in Liverpool discharging and loading cargo." In possession of the author.

In due course the cargo was finally discharged and we took on ballast for Baltimore. While our crew were not all Irishmen, they were all fond of Irish whiskey, and when we got outside the harbor I found that everybody on board was drunk except the captain and myself. You can imagine what it meant to start out with a crew in this condition and what a difficult matter it was to make sail. When I went forward to put them to work I found they were all in the forecastle, so I had to get in there and single-handedly persuade them to get out on deck that we might get sail on the vessel. Once I had them on deck I locked the forecastle doors so that there was no place for them to go. The second mate and the carpenter were both willing to help, but for the first few hours were of very little use. Under the conditions, it was necessary for us to go under short sail for a number of hours until the men sobered up enough to enable us to put all the canvas on the ship. In a day or two they were all straightened out and we had no more trouble during the passage.

At Baltimore the captain went up town and heard that some of the sailors who were persuaded out of the forecastle were going to get out a warrant for me, so he sent a towboat down and told me to get out of the way as quickly as I could. I stationed the old carpenter on the gangway to see that nobody came aboard while I got into my shore clothes. Just as I finished putting on my shirt the carpenter called out that there was a man coming down the dock whose looks he did not like. I came out of my room and climbed on board the tug with my coat and vest, collar and necktie in my hand. Just before I got over the rail the man coming down the wharf reached the dock and started to come up the gangway. When he was about half way up the carpenter went down to meet him and accidentally lurched into him, knocking him off the gangway down on the dock. The carpenter was very profuse in his apologies for his carelessness and held on to the man until he could get him brushed off, and then both went on board the ship. By that time the towboat with me on board was half a mile down the harbor, and I decided that it would be a good thing for me to go up to Philadelphia and keep out of sight for a few days, which I did. At the end of two weeks I received word that everything was all right and it was perfectly in order for me to rejoin the ship, which I proceeded to do.

At Baltimore Captain Young decided to leave the ship and take a rest, so Captain William Morton, who had practically retired from the sea but liked to take a passage every year or two so as to meet his old friends in the different ports, was placed in command. The ship was chartered to carry a cargo of blacksmith's coal from Baltimore to San Francisco. After the vessel was loaded we shipped a crew, the tugboat towing us out well clear of the Capes where we set sail and started on our long trip around the Horn.

At Sea again with another Captain

Captain Morton, who was about seventy years of age, was a fine type of the kindly old shipmaster. As he was only going to be in charge of the ship for one passage, and I had been there for several years, he made it very clear that he expected me to see to the running of the vessel with very little attention, especially with regard to details, from him. This suited me exactly, for I was young and ambitious, fond of the ship, familiar with every part of her, and I made up my mind that Captain Morton was going to have the pleasantest voyage he had ever had, and that I would see that he never was given an opportunity to ask for anything a second time, for no matter how busy I was, I always dropped everything to carry out any suggestion he made. The crew was fully up to average, in fact, better than we had had on some of the previous trips, so we had a very comfortable voyage except in one or two instances.

We had the usual weather until we struck the Southeast Trades in about twenty-five degrees, where we found perfect weather conditions, warm and pleasant with just a good whole-sail breeze. As we had to head well to the eastward to clear Cape Centro, it was necessary most of the time to have the yards sharp up, which meant that we had to give very little attention to trimming the sails, with that much more time to devote to putting the ship in order for the hard fight ahead of her when we reached the latitude of Cape Horn.

It is a disputed question as to whether animals are guided by instinct or reasoning. One experience we had that trip seemed to indicate that even chickens sometimes reason, for one morning after we had been at sea about fifty days, the captain was walking around the deck with me, and as we passed the chicken house he looked in and said, "Wouldn't it be a fine thing if we could have some fresh eggs for breakfast?" While chickens sometimes lay eggs at sea, owing to the fact that they get very little lime in their food, the old hen, almost invariably as soon as she has laid the egg, turns around and eats the shell.

Do Animals Reason?

After hearing the captain's wish I made up my mind that he was going to have an egg for breakfast, for I knew, from some of the sounds coming out of the chicken house, that several of the hens were laying. I therefore took a square box and put a canvas cover on it which I made very loose so that the weight of the hen would make it sag in the middle, and in the middle I cut a round hole somewhat larger than an egg, having first taken care to see that the bottom of the box was filled with shavings. Soon after the box was nailed into place, one of the hens proceeded to use it for a nest, and in due course stood up and started to cackle. Then she looked around for the egg but it was nowhere to be seen. Now that hen was perfectly certain that she had laid an egg, but could see no evidence of that fact. She looked all around, hopped down on the bottom of the chicken house, called the roosters to her assistance, and they looked everywhere and talked in chicken language about it, but still no egg!

In a little while I opened the door, stepped in, put my hand down the hole and took the egg out and took it to the galley so it could be cooked for the captain's breakfast next day, but that was the only egg that ever was laid in that box. Neither that hen nor any other ever undertook to use the box for a nest, and although it stayed there for the rest of the trip, it was never used again. So I think that we will have to admit that in this instance at least instinct was not the only factor to be considered, for although they did not lay eggs in the box they frequently laid them on deck, taking care to see that no one had a chance to get there until the hen who had laid the egg had eaten the shell covering it.

A further evidence that animals sometimes reason was told me by one of my old friends who was captain of a steamer running down along the Mexican coast. In order to have some cool drinking water, for there were no such things as refrigerators in those days, he had a Mexican olla hung up in one of the port holes where the breeze could blow over it and this let him have cool water to drink. On that voyage he had picked up a pet monkey which had the run of the cabin. The captain noticed that the monkey never seemed to drink any of the water that was provided for him, and for some time was at a loss to understand how the monkey could get along without drinking any of his water. One day he happened to look up and he saw the monkey standing on the olla in which he had thrust his tail and after letting it get thoroughly wet, pulled it out and licked the cool water off of it, satisfying his thirst in this way. Needless to say that that was his last opportunity to display his ingenuity.

Some years ago a friend of mine, who was working a small schooner through the Arctic Ocean, was up aloft looking for some open water which would enable him to get clear of the ice. While doing so, he noticed three polar bears who, by their peculiar actions, attracted his attention. They were apparently holding a conversation with their heads together, and then would look out over the ice in a certain direction. My friend followed their gaze and saw that they were looking at a seal apparently asleep on the edge of one of the floes. Suddenly one of the bears dove off of the ice and into the water. The other two bears waited for a short period and then walked in the direction of the seal, making very little attempt at concealment. As they approached, the seal raised his head and watched them, and when they came as close as he thought it was prudent to let them get, rolled off the ice into the water. Almost immediately my friend, who had been watching their movements carefully, noticed the third bear coming up over the edge of the ice with the seal in his mouth. As soon as he was safely up on the top of the floe, the bear proceeded to make a meal from his catch. The other two bears waited patiently until the bear who had caught the seal finished his repast and then they proceeded to eat what was left of the seal.

In all of these instances it would seem that the different so-called "dumb" animals had displayed a certain amount of reasoning power.

Man Overboard

After losing the Southeast Trades we had the usual changeable weather until we were down in the latitude of Cape Horn, where we had the gales and heavy seas which are always to be found in that latitude. One morning when we were sailing close-hauled with main upper topsail and mainsail, the bosun sent one of the sailors up to the foretopgallant yard to put an extra gasket around the sail in order to prevent its going adrift. Suddenly I heard a cry from some of the men on deck who were looking over the side, and there was the sailor who had fallen from the topgallant yard to the sea, a distance of about 150 feet. I immediately gave orders to call all hands and throw the main yard aback, at the same time telling them to get a gantline on the fore yardarm so we could get out the boat. While these orders were being carried out I had thrown the life buoy in the sea near where the man was, but he made no effort to take hold of it so I presumed that the distance he had fallen had probably stunned him. I remember very distinctly going on top of the house to see that the gantline was properly fast to lift the boat out, and while this was being done I took off my coat and slippers and put them down, saying to them as I did so, "I do not believe I will ever need you again."

We swung the boat out and, taking four men with me, started to search for the man who had gone overboard. The sea was very heavy, so heavy in fact that we could not go in the trough of it at all, but had to be careful to work slowly away with the bow of the boat heading the sea. We could find no trace of the man and, after looking for him about five hours, slowly worked our way back to the ship. As we got in close under the stern, I noticed that the carpenter was standing on top of the wheelhouse using a bucket to pour oil on the sea and so make it possible for us to get back. It was very dangerous approaching the ship. As she rose and fell, I saw we had to keep the boat well off to avoid being swamped. I finally got all the boat's crew back on board except myself and then had them hoist the boat up with me in her so I could keep her clear of the side of the ship as she came up. My reception when I reached the deck was not very cordial, for Captain Morton made it very clear to me that he did not approve of my going out in a small boat in any such sea as was running then, and issued very definite instructions for me never to do it again. Fortunately, it was never necessary for me to run the risk of disobeying these instructions. This was the only sailor that was ever lost overboard from any ship I was on during all the years I spent at sea.

We had rather a hard time in the vicinity of the Cape, and it was necessary for us to go down to 60 degrees south before we could get far enough to the westward to allow us to clear the coast of Tierra del Fuego, and start north. Once clear of the Cape we soon ran into moderate weather and unbent the heavy sails we had used around Cape Horn. One night when we were going along with a fair breeze about the latitude of Valparaiso, while I had the watch from eight to twelve, I became uneasy for some unknown reason and commenced to take in the light sails. The glass had fallen a little but not enough to warrant the feeling of uneasiness I had. I finally took in all the skysails, royals, and topgallant sails, which brought the rig down to an extent suitable for quite a strong breeze. I called the captain before I left the deck at midnight and told him what I had done. I said there was apparently no reason for taking such precautions but that I simply felt uneasy and had taken the canvas off her. His reply was, "If you feel like taking canvas off, I think it is about time to do it, for I have never seen you take in any canvas before it was necessary, so tell the second mate when he relieves you to be careful and be on the lookout for change in the weather." I reported these instructions to the second mate, who had sailed for many years in the North Atlantic packet ships and was a thorough seaman. We had been together for two or three voyages and, strange to say, had always remained the best of friends, which is not always the case between men occupying our respective positions.

After being relieved I turned in and, as in those days sailors did not wear pajamas or night shirts, I simply took off my slippers, trousers and outer shirt, for in weather of that kind I never wore stockings while at sea. I had only been asleep a short time when I was awakened by the ship giving a

Sudden Storm

sudden lurch to leeward. A moment afterwards the second mate stuck his head in the door and said, "For God's sake come out here, sir, she has struck end first!"

On reaching the deck I glanced aloft and saw that he had loosed several of the light sails but hadn't had a chance to set them. One glance showed what the situation was so I immediately ran to the forecastle where my watch was asleep, jumped in and grabbed hold of the men by anything I could reach — hands, feet, hair, or whatever my hand came to first, told them what the situation was and drove them out ahead of me. As I ran along the deck I told the second mate to look out for the main and mizzen, I would look out for the jibboom and foremast.

After four hours hard work in taking some of the canvas off the ship and securing the remains of those of the sails which had blown away, I went aft to see how she was heading and what conditions were in that part of the ship. While I was doing so, the cabin door opened and Captain Morton came out and remarked that we had had quite a breeze. He asked how many sails we had lost, and I told him fourteen.

As I came out of my room without stopping to put on anything but my slippers, I had been working for four hours with only a single garment on, but the weather was warm and I had been too busy to pay any attention to what I was wearing. The old captain looked me over and said, "Squall blow away all your clothes?"

I replied, "No, sir, but I didn't stop to put any on."

He told me he could think of no better use for five minutes at that time than for me to use it in putting on my ordinary clothing.

After we reached port we heard that two or three vessels had been partially dismasted in approximately the same latitude, one of which had to put in to Valparaiso to refit. It was evidently a freak storm of which there were no suitable indications. Had we not replaced our Cape Horn canvas with the old fair weather sails which gave way before the force of the gale, I am sure we too would have lost some spars.

Thirty Men Confined For Four Months

Soon after this experience we picked up the Southeast Trades, which gave us a fair wind for the point at which we wanted to cross the equator. After losing the trades we had the usual experience of working our way through the doldrums, but as has been noted, the *Wakefield* was particularly well equipped to navigate this difficult stretch of water because she was so lofty that, if there was any wind at all, her upper sails caught it and thus gave her the necessary headway. On leaving the doldrums we soon picked up the Northeast Trades, which meant fine sailing weather.

I had an experience while we were in the trades which shows what may happen when you confine thirty men in such a small space for four months. One morning while the men were hauling braces I was standing on the weather side watching to see when the time came to tell them to belay. There had been no discussion, nothing but the routine orders had been issued, all with reference to which rope they were to pull on, and I was standing carelessly watching for the proper time to tell them that the braces were tight enough, when I saw one of the crew come over toward the side of the deck where I was standing. Suddenly, without a word, he made a lunge at me with a sheath knife. I was young and agile and sprang to one side. The knife went through the shirt which was all I had on, but it did not touch the skin. I turned to the sailor and told him to throw his knife overboard. He looked at me in an uncertain way and I repeated the command, whereupon he threw the knife overboard. I told him to go down and go on with his work and not let us have any more of such foolishness, and there the matter rested as far as I was concerned.

I can give no explanation as to his motive in making the attack except that he had become momentarily mentally unbalanced and did not realize what he was doing. I dismissed the matter entirely from my mind — he had not hurt me, so there was no harm done. After breakfast in my watch below I was walking along the weather side of the house when I heard some loud talking at the other side of the deck. I thought that if anybody around there was entitled to do any loud talking I was the individual, so I hurried up to see what was going on. As I did so, I saw that the old captain had grabbed this man who had attempted to stab me with his knife and was just about ready to strike him, but before he could do so I had made one long running jump and had both arms around the old gentleman and persuaded him that there was no necessity for his concerning himself any further in the matter, that no harm had been done, and if he would go into the cabin I was sure I had a book which he had not seen which I thought he would like to read. The old gentleman was very indignant, but I finally persuaded him that he needn't worry, that the matter was all over and no damage done. I merely tell this story to show that perhaps some of the tales we hear of what happens on shipboard are not always caused by harsh treatment of the men.

Old sailor men have a superstition that it is dangerous for anyone to sleep in the moonlight. While I have never seen any ill effects from this experience, I have heard men whose reputation for telling the truth was very good make the definite statement that they had seen sailors who had slept in the moonlight on their watch on deck during the warm weather of the tropics, or when running down the trades, have their faces all drawn out of shape. On this trip out the second mate, who was a firm believer in the ill effects which might result from this, saw two of the boys in his watch lying on the main deck sound asleep with the moonlight shining full on their faces. He had the bosun draw him several buckets of water, and then stepping close up to the boys threw them on their faces as quickly as he could, at the same time crying out to them, "Swim, you rascals, swim!" The boys were so impressed by the amount of water around them that they immediately started trying to do so. As a result of their experience, they never gave the second mate any further trouble by sleeping in the moonlight.

We made the usual run through the Southeast Trades and crossed the line as we had planned to do at 110 degrees west longitude. Soon after doing so we ran out of the trades and into the doldrums where we had light baffling airs, calm and rainy weather. After a week of this, we picked up the Northeast Trades which, of course, drove us well to the westward. Soon after losing the trades we picked up the westerly winds and headed in towards San Francisco, arriving there 27 April 1887 after a voyage of 142 days from Baltimore.

Upon discharging the cargo of coal, Captain Morton gave up command of the *Cyrus Wakefield*, turning her over to Captain Gleason Young, who had come overland to rejoin the ship. There were very few charters offering at that time because the wheat crop for the year had not yet been harvested, so the ship was laid up over in Sausalito, only the captain, carpenter, cook, and myself being retained to look after the vessel. A few weeks after we anchored in the bay off Sausalito, Captain Young was ordered to go to Manila and take command of the *R. D. Rice*, a ship belonging to the same owners whose captain was ill and wanted to come home, so I was left in charge of the vessel for the time being.

At this time the coasting trade was very active and a good many of the deep-water men, as we called those who were in the Cape Horn trade, joined the coasters. At that time I was barely twenty-five years of age and looked to be about twenty-two. One day one of the owners of a line of coasting vessels

Master of the *Cyrus Wakefield*

whom I had met ashore in Sausalito a number of times, suggested that I go over and see one of his captains whom he knew wanted a mate. I did so. The captain of this little vessel, about 700 tons, looked me over and decided I was too young for the position, but told me if I would get a little more experience and come to him some other time, if he had an opening he would be glad to consider me for the position. I was thoroughly disgusted with the result of my attempt to join one of the coasting vessels and decided I would go back to the deep-water ships where I was at home.

About nine months later, after I had just broken the world's record from San Francisco to Europe and back again as master of a ship three times the size of this small bark, I walked into a ship chandler's office where a number of captains were sitting and was asked if I knew Captain _____. I said, "Oh, yes, nine months ago when I applied for a position as mate with him he told me that I lacked experience enough to go mate of a bark of that size, but if I would come back in two or three years and he had an opening he would be glad to talk to me."

You can imagine the exclamations this brought out from the different members of the crowd, for in those days the size of the ship he commanded, to a certain extent determined the master's standing in the world and it is therefore easy to understand the difference in position between the master of a 700-ton bark and the master of a three-skysail-yard full-rigged ship, especially one that had just made such a record passage. The old man slipped out of the room in about five minutes, and for a number of years always crossed the street whenever he saw me coming towards him.

About the first of June, while we lay at Sausalito, a representative of the stevedores came alongside the ship with a crew of men and handed me a letter from Captain Chapman, the agent of the ship in San Francisco, in which I was instructed to get up anchor and bring the ship over to section four of the seawall. Promptly at nine o'clock the next morning I was in Captain Chapman's office and reported that the ship was at the seawall as per his instructions. Captain Chapman told me that the ship had been chartered for Liverpool and that I was going out as master of her, for me to arrange for a crew and the necessary provisions, and also to have the ship put in order to receive a grain cargo.

I do not believe it would mean as much to me today if I were told that I had been made president of the United States, as did that simple statement by Captain Chapman that I was to go out as master of that fine ship, for I did not believe then, nor do I now, that any finer vessel was sailing under the American flag at that time. You can imagine what it meant to a boy of twenty-five to be given this splendid opportunity.

After taking in the necessary stiffening at the seawall in order to permit the ship to safely make the trip to Port Costa where we were to receive the balance of our cargo, we towed up to that point and completed the loading of the vessel. We left San Francisco on 28 May 1887 and arrived in Liverpool 116 days later.

To Liverpool and Back

Going up the Irish Sea on our way to Liverpool, we picked up one of the big ocean tugboats off Tuskar Light on the Irish Coast. In our negotiations, the captain of the towboat kept calling me Captain Morton, and as he knew Captain Morton was an old trader to the port and knew what he ought to pay for such a tow, we made a very satisfactory arrangement. My name had not been put on the papers until the day we sailed, so it was quite easy to understand why the towboat captain should think that Captain Morton was still master of the vessel. When we reached the Mersey and anchored, the towboat came alongside to take me ashore. When I was dressed and ready to leave the ship, I went over on the tugboat and reported, went up on the bridge and told the captain everything was alright and he could go in to the dock. He informed me that he was waiting for Captain Morton. I told him that Captain Morton was not in command of the vessel, but that I held that position at that time. I wish I could adequately describe the look on the captain's face when he found that he had been dealing with a mere boy instead of an old seasoned trader to that port.

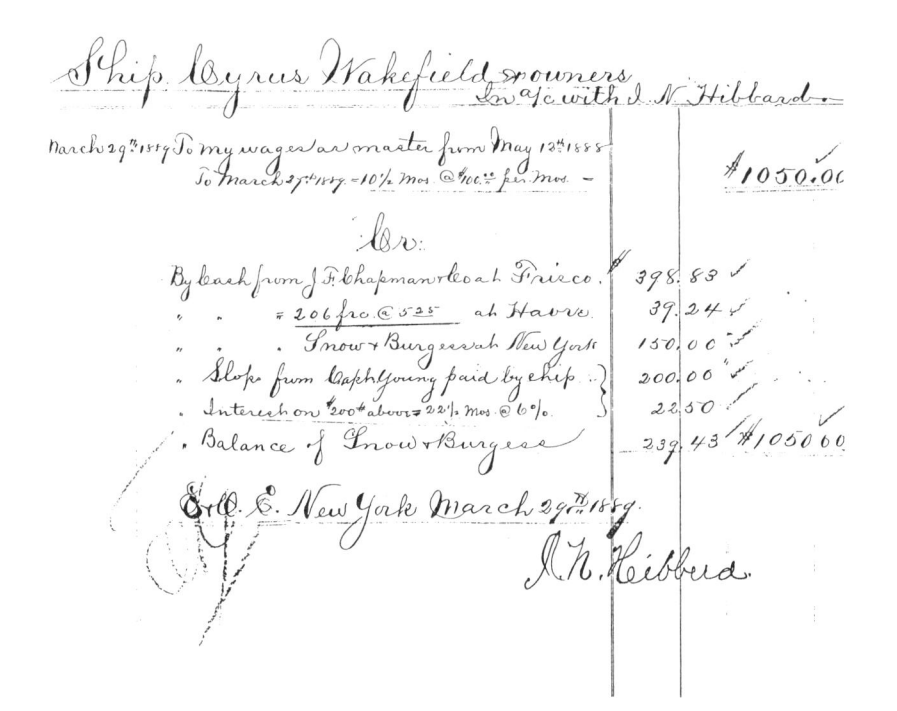

Capt. Hibberd's accounts as master of the *Cyrus Wakefield*, 12 May 1888 to 29 March 1889. This and other papers documenting the operation of the *Cyrus Wakefield* are in the Samuel Watts Collection at the G. W. Blunt White Library, Mystic Seaport Museum.

It is interesting to see what a change the position of an individual can take in a short time. While the *Wakefield* was laying off Sausalito waiting for a charter, there was another ship moored not far away doing the same thing. On this latter vessel the captain had his family, consisting of his wife, twenty-year-old daughter, and a son fourteen years of age. They all greeted me very pleasantly when we met on the ferryboat running between San Francisco and Sausalito or on shore at Sausalito, but they would have been very much surprised had I presumed to step over the line of demarcation between a mate and a captain and call upon them some evening aboard their ship. As it happened, this other ship was chartered, loaded and sailed while we were still laying at anchor in Sausalito. A few days after this ship sailed, the *Wakefield* was chartered for Liverpool and I was appointed master. It was three weeks after the sailing of the *Standard* before we cleared the harbor of San Francisco. When we arrived at Liverpool I inquired for the *Standard* but found that she had not arrived. Our vessel was half discharged before the latter vessel arrived in Liverpool. Ascertaining the dock she was to enter, I went down to wait her arrival. As soon as she was made fast I stepped aboard and was cordially greeted by the captain and his family. In the five months which had elapsed since the *Standard* left San Francisco, our positions had been reversed somewhat, for I was then the master of a 2,000-ton ship while Captain Percy's vessel, the *Standard*, only measured 1,500 tons, and I was therefore quite a welcome guest whenever I had the opportunity of calling.

We discharged our California wheat cargo in fine order, and as the ship was chartered for a cargo of coal back to San Francisco, proceeded over to the coal dock for the outward cargo. I had given the mate instructions as to just how I wanted the ship trimmed. When I came down, all ready to go to sea, I found that she was two inches more by the head than my instructions called for. When I asked the mate why he had not followed my wishes, he replied that the foreman of the loading gang wanted to put the coal in forward instead of going to the trouble of calling for a switch of crews to the after hatch where they belonged. I told him to pack up his clothes, that if he was going to take orders from the foreman instead of me there was no place for him on board the ship. I told the second mate to go forward and take charge of the forecastle head as he was going mate of the ship on that trip.

I stepped out on the dock where there were a lot of old sailors waiting for a possibility of an opening, and asked them if there was anyone there who could go second mate of the ship. One little old chap spoke up and said that he was a second mate, so I told him to put his clothes on board. On this outward trip I was the only person on board ship who had any knowledge of navigation. Both the mate and the second mate were thoroughly competent practical seamen, but that was the limit of their ability.

Mirages at Sea

We left Liverpool on 21 October. Shortly before we reached the latitude of Cape Horn, one clear afternoon the sailors who were working aloft reported land on the lee bow. I could not possibly conceive how that could be for if my position were correct, the only land in that locality was the Falkland Islands, a long way to the eastward, for the course I was steering should carry me down just to the eastward of Staten Island. After sailing on for a while the apparent land loomed up clearer and every one on board the ship was convinced that we were running right into a bight, as the land by that time had shown up on both bows. As this happened just before nightfall, I headed the ship to the eastward and kept her on that course all night. In the morning there was no land in sight, so I hauled back to the westward, and it was not until late that afternoon that we made the lower end of Staten Island. On checking up the distance run I found that my chronometers were correct and that what we all had taken for land was only a mirage. However, the mistake had lengthened our passage just twenty-four hours.

This experience was of much value to me some years later when I was a passenger on a steamer going to Nome, Alaska. One bright afternoon land suddenly appeared ahead. Among the passengers were many miners who had been up there before who claimed to be able to identify the different points of land. The captain asked me if I could locate any particular point. I told him that I had never seen that land before. This surprised him very much, for at that time I was supposed to have a rather complete knowledge of all the coast of Alaska in that vicinity.

In answer to my inquiry as to how far away Nome was according to his record at noon that day, he said, "Two hundred and forty miles." As the weather was clear and there were no signs of discoloration, I suggested that it would be perfectly safe to go on for a while at least. After we had been proceeding toward the land, which seemed to come out more clearly for an hour, the different points of which many of our passengers claimed to identify, it commenced to fade away and in an hour had completely disappeared, much to the chagrin of the different individuals who had insisted upon their ability to identify the various headlands. We made Nome next morning, showing that the captain's position of the day before had been correct. This land looked so real that I am sure it would have deceived me as badly as it did all the others had it not been for my experience years before in the *Wakefield* off Staten Island.

Not long after leaving the heavy weather off the Cape, we spoke a ship which proved to be the *Sea King*. We hoisted our number and his reply was "cannot understand your signals." As he was near enough to read them easily, I could not understand why there should be any difficulty about it, so hauled down the code flag which gave the name of the ship and her hailing port, and proceeded to spell her name out letter by letter. On looking up the name of the vessel in the latest maritime register I had on board, I found that the *Sea King* had left New York for San Francisco before we reached Liverpool, therefore it was easy to understand why he could not believe that the code letters which we had hoisted could possibly be correct when his latest paper showed him they belonged to a vessel bound to Liverpool.

We had the usual fine weather through the trades in the South Pacific. One day while all hands were busy removing all traces of the rough weather we had passed through in rounding Cape Horn, I was sitting reading in the cabin when I heard a peculiar cry. I knew at once that it meant someone had fallen overboard and I hurried on deck. Noticing that all the men were gazing over the rail toward the stern, I looked in that direction and saw a man swimming in the water. We always kept two life buoys fastened to the rail with twine so that in an emergency anyone could break them adrift. I immediately seized one and threw it out in the water near where the man was swimming. I then gave the necessary orders to bring the ship up in the wind and put the main yard back, at the same time ordering them to get out one of the life boats.

I then went to the compass and took a bearing showing how the man bore from the ship. When the ship came up in the wind, instead of being astern, the man was well off on the starboard quarter, but this made no difference in his bearing by compass, so by the time the boat was in the water the man was entirely out of sight. By standing on top of the wheelhouse and signalling to the boat to keep on the line of bearing which I had taken, the boat went straight to where the man was, picked him up and brought him back, none the worse for his experience. As the weather and water were both warm, what little discomfort he had felt was easily taken care of by giving him a glass of whiskey, and I am not sure that almost any of the other men would not have been willing to go through the same experience for a similar cure-all. It has always been a matter of satisfaction to me that I had the foresight to go to the compass and take a bearing on the man in the water, otherwise I am sure we would never have been able to find him, for a person is soon lost sight of in the open sea.

We arrived in San Francisco Bay very early in the morning. When Captain Chapman arrived at his office he found a message from the lookout on Point Lobos saying the ship was passing in. The captain telephoned the station saying there must be a mistake, the *Wakefield* couldn't be here for thirty days. The lookout replied that, "Mistaken or not, sir, she is at anchor in the bay and her master is coming ashore." And in a little while I walked into the captain's office, taking off my hat as I greeted him. Captain Chapman was a very dignified, impressive looking gentleman, standing about six feet two inches and weighing approximately 250 pounds. As I walked up to his desk, the old gentleman arose, took off his hat and said, "Put on your hat, sir, we take off our hat to you these days."

It is hard to conceive what a compliment I felt that to be, for in my eyes Captain Chapman was the most important man in the world, being an owner in forty-eight American vessels.

A few days after our arrival, I was coming out of Captain Chapman's office when I met the mate of a ship we had seen off Cape Horn, coming down the hall. As soon as he saw me he started back surprised, and I asked him what was the matter. He replied that he thought I had been lost. In answer to my inquiry as to why he had that impression, he asked me if I remembered the night I saw them off Cape Horn. I told him that I had a very distinct recollection of that evening. He said, "Well, when morning came and you were nowhere in sight, we thought you had gone under, for it seemed to us that nothing that was built of wood and iron could stand the driving you were giving that ship that night."

I told him that I had not gone under but that I had gone on ahead. It had been overcast for the last three or four days for the run from the line to San Francisco and I had not been able to get a sight to determine accurately what my position was, having to depend entirely on dead reckoning. About ten o'clock the night before we arrived at San Francisco, I told the mate that when the watch came on deck at twelve o'clock to take in all the light sails, haul out the courses, and lay the main topsail to the mast. After he had all the sail clewed up but not made fast, the fog suddenly cleared away and I found I was right in mid-channel of the entrance to San Francisco. The topgallant sails and courses were immediately set, leaving the skysails and royals furled. Not long after we picked up a pilot and sailed into San Francisco in the early morning without having had to employ a tug. It would not have been possible for me to make a better landfall had I been able to get all of the sights I wished to.

Life in the old ships in those days was a constant battle of wits between nature and the man in command. If you took in sail too soon you made a slow passage; if you kept it on too long and lost it you were handicapped when the weather moderated, and this tended to lengthen your passage. One fine old shipmaster summed up the situation very completely when he said, "Any fool can carry sail until it blows away, the seaman is the man who can carry it to the last minute, then take it in safely and have it ready to set as soon as the weather moderates." And it was this constant lookout as to just how long you could keep canvas on the ship and yet get it in safely that enabled some shipmasters to make quicker passages than others who were otherwise clearly as competent.

There is a yarn told of the ship captains of earlier days that when they reached port after a long voyage they took all of the medicines that were left in the medicine chest and put them into one bottle, and whenever one of the sailors complained of being sick and they were not able to diagnose the complaint, always gave him a dose from this bottle, feeling sure that there must be something in the mixture which would be of benefit to him. This is probably one of the many yarns about life on shipboard in the early days for which there is no foundation. Certainly there was no such method practiced by any of the shipmasters of my day.

Along the West Coast

After discharging a cargo of coal which was consigned to the Pacific Improvement Company, it being too early in the season to be able to secure a grain cargo, we left on 8 March [1888] for Seattle for another cargo of coal. We had a quick run up the coast and very little delay in loading, so were able to leave Seattle 12 April for San Francisco, making the trip down in seven days. As the weather was cloudy part of the way, I was not able to get observations the last two days. Dead reckoning put me down near Point Reyes early in the morning of the sixth day out from Seattle, so I thought I would go up aloft, thinking I might be able to see over the fog which was hanging over the water.

As I reached the fore skysail yard I saw a vessel with all sails set straight ahead of us, so made up my mind that everything was clear ahead. Coming down from aloft I started to walk back and forth across the topgallant forecastle. I had not been doing this very long before I heard the sound of breakers straight ahead, and made up my mind that although it might be all right for the other ship, it was no place for me, so immediately tacked and stood off shore.

The next morning when we sailed into San Francisco, I found that a ship coming down just a day ahead of me had run ashore with all sails set, and the ship that I had seen was this vessel hard and fast aground. Had I not by chance stepped on the forecastle when I came down from aloft, we might possibly have done the same thing. As it was, we reached San Francisco safely on 19 April. We discharged our Seattle cargo and sailed again on 15 May for another cargo.

We did not do so well going up the coast this time because of the head winds we encountered, but as it was summertime the breezes were moderated so that the trip was a pleasant one, if somewhat longer than I liked. I had been on deck most of the two days before we passed in by Tatoosh Island [Cape Flattery] where, fortunately, we found a fair wind which let us head a straight course up the Strait of Juan de Fuca.

I had rather an unusual experience here which has helped me to understand seemingly unaccountable mistakes in judgment made by others at various times. As the weather was fine, we were running along with the yards nearly square and it was an easy matter to keep the ship on her course. Just before we reached Dungeness, I noticed that we were heading inside of the buoy off the point, and while I realized fully that there was not sufficient water for us to pass inside the buoy, it required a strong mental effort on my part to issue the necessary orders to change the course sufficiently to take her outside the buoy where she would be in the proper channel. Had I not changed the course I am sure we would have gone hard and fast aground, and I would never have been able to explain why I made the mistake. As a matter of fact, it was just one of those times when, probably due to fatigue in this case, the mind failed to function as it should. I have always been very glad, however, that I was able to overcome the impulse to let the ship continue on what I knew to be a dangerous course.

It has seemed to me a number of times when I hear of people who have made mistakes for which there is no apparent excuse, that perhaps the real reason was that their brain failed to function properly at the critical moment, and I think this is one of the factors which will always have to be taken into account where the human element is considered.

There was much unemployment on Puget Sound while we were there, and an attempt was made by persuasion and threatening to induce the sailors to leave the vessel so that the entire loading could be done by stevedores from the shore. I was not willing that this should happen and managed to keep the disturbing element from interfering with the crew. One night when we were working both ends of the ship, the longshoremen, who were working in the after end of the ship while the crew were handling the coal that came down the forward end, made a determined effort to carry their point, but as the mate was on deck and I was sitting on the coal in the hold, they were not able to reach the men, for every time one of them made an attempt to sneak forward he was advised that that was just about as far as it was safe for him to go. We kept this up until morning and thus were able to frustrate any attempt to interfere with the men.

The day that we left Seattle, while in tow of the tug, I noticed a fracas about the galley door so went forward to see what the trouble was. I found a very indignant cook who was outraged because the sailors had returned some nice pumpkin pies which he had made. As it happened, the pumpkins were some I had picked out for myself, but as there was danger of their spoiling, the cook good-naturedly thought he would divide them up with the crew, with a result that was far from what he had anticipated.

There was one sailor in the crew who had been with me for a couple of voyages, so I sent for him and asked him why the men objected to the pies, for

A Question of Taste

as far as I could see there could be no possible objection to them. The explanation was that coasting sailors objected to vegetable pies. I thereupon told the cook that I thought he was not entitled to any sympathy, for if he had kept the pumpkins to make pies for me, as originally planned, he would have had no trouble with the sailors, because all the rest of the food was entirely satisfactory. I think that some of our Down East friends who are so fond of pumpkin pie would say that these sailors didn't know a good thing when they saw it.

There were several ships in port and each one of us had to wait our proper turn. One day while we were waiting we decided to invite some of our friends to go out sailing with us. One of the ships had a life boat which was especially well fitted for this purpose, so we used her. There were five captains in the party, each one of whom was master of a vessel at that time in the harbor.

After we had been out a while we ran into a squall which necessitated careful handling if we wanted to avoid an accident. The amusing part of the experience was that everybody issued orders and for a few moments nobody did anything. We soon snapped out of this, however, and did what was necessary to see that the boat was properly handled. After it was over, we all realized how serious the situation might have been, and thereafter whenever we went out sailing, determined before we started who was to be the captain of the ship for the afternoon and so avoided any danger of repeating this experience.

Some of my friends on shore considered it quite a treat to come down and have dinner with me. One day there were a number of members of the Women's Christian Temperance Union dining with me. As it was a special occasion, the cook had made a large plum duff with plenty of sauce to go with it. Both the plum duff and the sauce proved to be a favorite with everyone, and the ladies were quite curious to know just what the sauce was flavored with. As the flavoring happened to be old Jamaica rum, I was placed in rather an embarrassing position, for I knew if I told them just what it was they would not have looked back on their dinner with the pleasure and satisfaction I wanted them to have, so I explained that the cook, who was a Frenchman, had many recipes of his own for making attractive sauces, and then, at the first opportunity, sent word to him on no account to explain to anybody just how the sauce was flavored on that particular day.

On the *Wakefield* we had a fore topgallant mast of Norway pine which, although tough, was inclined to buckle forward when we were carrying jib topsails in a strong breeze. I used to look up at that topgallant mast when the breeze freshened, and if it was not daytime I kept the sail on as long as I thought I could without danger of taking the topgallant mast over the side. Many a time at night when the breeze freshened, I have left the quarterdeck, walked forward and looked up toward that topgallant mast, although that mast was 140 feet from the deck and I could not see more than twenty feet. While I knew exactly what it was doing and could have drawn a picture of it, as long as I could not see the mast bending under the strain of the sail, I would walk aft satisfied that it would be all right to carry it a little longer. If it had been daylight and I could have actually seen what was taking place, I am sure the sail would have been hauled down many times.

We left Seattle 15 July [1888], and after a quick trip down the coast, reached San Francisco 22 July. After discharging the cargo of coal from Seattle, the ship was chartered to load wheat for Havre and after taking on her cargo sailed for that port on 29 August. We had a fine run down to the line, which we crossed in 120 degrees west, and picked up the Southeast Trades which we held until about 25 degrees south. As they were somewhat to the southward, we were kept well to the westward, making Pitcairn Island, where we stopped one afternoon and secured some fruit and fresh vegetables in exchange for clothing, books, and such medical supplies and hardware as we could spare. Having in mind the experience we had on my first visit, I again took good care to see that there was no opportunity for a repetition of what occurred at that time.

We had a fine run around the Cape as we were down there late in October, which was their spring. We found the Southeast Trades in the South Atlantic well to the northward, which made it necessary for us to stand over to the African coast much farther than we usually did. In fact, it was necessary to go over into one degree east longitude before the wind hauled sufficiently to the southward of east for our purpose.

I found that the course from where we were when the wind changed to where I wanted to cross the equator would take us right by St. Helena. As we had a man who had been laid up for some time I decided to stop there and have a doctor come off and examine him. We arrived there early one Sunday morning. The weather was very fine and clear, so we stood in fairly close and put out a boat. Leaving the ship in charge of the mate, I went ashore to get the doctor. Our arrival created quite an excitement. It was the first time any ship from San Francisco had been there. In fact, they did not know where San Francisco was and I had to explain just what part of North America we had sailed from. The doctor went over with me, and after making an examination of the man stated that he could not recommend any treatment which would be more satisfactory than the one I had been giving him. Accordingly, I continued treating the man just as I had been previously, and I am glad to say that by the time we had reached Havre he had completely recovered.

We arrived at Havre 20 December, after a passage of 113 days. As it was just before the Christmas holidays I decided to pay a visit to Paris as soon as I had the ship's business in condition to let me be away for a few days. I did the usual sightseeing there, going through the Louvre, Hotel Cluny, went to see the grave of Abelard and Heloise, and in fact did as much sightseeing as I could in the few days at my disposal. Christmas Eve I went to the Grand Opera House and heard Patti and Jean de Reske in *Romeo and Juliet*, a gorgeous performance. After the opera I went to the students ball in the Latin Quarter, a very gay affair. This wound up my visit to Paris and I went back to the ship in Havre.

Le Havre

In checking up my accounts I found that after paying all of my bills, although our freight rate had been 27 shillings, 6 pence, there would be enough left to send to Captain Watts, the owner, a draft for $15,000. In due course I received a letter from Captain Watts saying he had received my letter with the draft enclosed, but did not see where I got the money. In reply I acknowledged receipt of his letter telling of having received the draft, and that he need not worry, the money was all his. When I think of the detail in which the modern ships render their accounts now, I often wonder what the owners would think of receiving such a reply.

In fact, all during my experience as a master, I never sent the owners a single voucher covering the expenses. All I did was to send a statement showing the amount of freight money received and the items for whatever I had used was spent, but in no instance was there any supporting voucher and no one ever questioned the accuracy of the account. I am sure this was the experience of practically all shipmasters of that time and it is a tribute to the confidence placed in them by their owner.

There was no freight available from Havre for New York, so we sailed for that port in ballast 10 January [1889], arriving there 15 February. The weather was very cold when we made the Atlantic coast and the ship was badly iced up going into New York. A few days after we docked, Captain Young, who had completed his voyage with the *R. D. Rice* and had been visiting at home for some time, came down and took command of the ship. Soon after his arrival, after I had explained to him just what the situation was, he asked me how soon I would be ready to go down to Thomaston to get Mrs. Young and the children, including a baby a few months old who had been named for me. I told him I thought that he had better go after the family and I would gladly look after the ship while he was gone. This did not meet with his approval and he insisted that I go down and get Mrs. Young and the children and bring them to New York.

The Long Walk

You can imagine this was quite a task for a man twenty-seven years old who had never had any family experience. However, I did as he requested and we started from Thomaston with all my pockets full of milk bottles and other necessities for my namesake. We got along very well as far as Boston, where Mrs. Young spent the night with some relatives while I went to a hotel, meeting her the next morning. Soon after we started, the young man became very restless, so it was necessary for me to walk up and down the car with him in order to keep him quiet. This I did for practically the whole trip from Boston to New York, and I often refer to that experience as the time I walked from Boston to New York. However, we reached the destination safely and I was able to turn his family over to Captain Young in good order and condition, receiving a clean receipt therefor.

Master of the *Alexander Gibson*

After closing up my affairs with the *Wakefield* I paid a visit to my old home outside of Philadelphia, and then went over land to San Francisco where I took command of the *Alexander Gibson* 19 July 1889. I found the ship had been chartered for Liverpool and after completing her loading, getting a crew and all the supplies necessary, we sailed on 4 September 1889, and after a passage of 129 days reached Liverpool 11 January 1890.

Nothing unusual occurred during this trip other than some exceptionally heavy weather off Cape Horn. As the wind was fair we ran for several days under the lower main topsail with the sheets well slacked off. It is a very impressive sight at night to see these long heavy seas all alight with a phosphorescent glow go rolling by. We saw very few other vessels during the passage, and no land at all after leaving San Francisco until we reached the Irish coast.

Our two chronometers did not agree at all on this trip, and just before we reached Cape Clear, Mr. Johnson, the mate, and I were commenting on this fact, I had much more confidence in one than I had in the other because according to the reckoning of one of them we should have been ashore on the northwestern coast of France, while the other put us where I wanted to be, which was in the longitude of Cape Clear. The mate suggested that I take the average of the two chronometers. I explained to him that if I did that I knew I would be wrong, because I was sure we were not aground on the French coast, and therefore I determined to pin my faith on the other one. The result justified me in taking this position because we made the landfall just when and where I had expected to find it.

In these days of radio signals and directions finders, it is difficult to make anyone realize what a chronometer meant to a shipmaster when he knew it was the one instrument on which he had to depend absolutely if he was to take the lives and the property under his charge safely to their destination. When you think of the thousands of these instruments which were in use and the very few occasions in which they failed to justify the confidence placed in them, one cannot help but feel a sincere respect, almost affection, for these reliable old friends. On my departure from San Francisco for Havre my Negus chronometer showed that it was gaining at the rate of one-tenth of a second a day. On our arrival in Havre 113 days later, the chronometer was sent ashore for re-rating and when it came back just before we sailed for New York, it had the same rate. Such extreme accuracy as this is, of course, not always to be expected in any instrument no matter how high its quality.

I sailed on 13 February for New York, arriving there 29 March 1890. It was winter time and I knew that if we took the northern passage we would encounter heavy westerly winds and rough seas. I decided to take the southern route, feeling sure that we would not be more than four or five days longer on the trip, and the wear and tear on the vessel would much more than make up for the extra time. We made the run across in forty-four days, which was a better passage than some of the other vessels leaving about the same time were able to make going by the northern route, and in addition, the ship was not subjected to the hard usage which the northern route entailed.

I found we were chartered to load a general cargo for San Francisco, which proved to be made up of every variety of merchandise from steel rails to feather dusters, brooms, furniture, dry goods, and every commodity the people of California had any use for. As soon as the cargo was all on board we shipped a crew and started for our long trip by way of the Cape. New York is in longitude 75 degrees west and it was therefore necessary to steer well to the southward and eastward so that we would be able to cross the equator in longitude 30 degrees and so keep clear of St. Roque, the northeastern extremity of Brazil. On this voyage I found the Northeast Trades had very little northing in them, which prevented us from getting as

Ship *Alex. Gibson*, 2,121 tons, 247.3x42.6x29.6, built by Edward O'Brien at Thomaston, Maine, 1877. Taken from the New York waterfront, this photograph shows the *Gibson* under tow in the East River, just south of the Brooklyn Bridge. Courtesy of the Peabody Museum of Salem.

far to the eastward as we wanted to. After we ran out of the Northeast Trades, in addition to the light airs and calms of the doldrums, we found a strong westerly current setting.

Knowing our position, I was on the lookout for the northern coast of Brazil, as I knew we were getting close to that locality. Glancing over the side one morning I noticed a difference in the color of the water, so had some drawn up and on tasting it found it very nearly fresh. I knew at once that we were right off the mouth of the Amazon so tacked ship and headed to the northward as I did not want to run any risk of getting too close to the Brazilian shore. I was surprised to find that in this vicinity there was no westerly current such as we had encountered a day or two before. Whether this was due to the strength of the waters discharged by the Amazon or not, I could not say. However, we were soon able to work well clear of the land and find a breeze which enabled us to keep well clear of St. Roque and so let us go on our way down to Cape Horn.

Stormy Passages

After leaving the trades the winds gradually grew stronger as we reached the latitude of the Cape. We sighted Cape St. John and the northeast corner of Staten Island, and then for three weeks it was a constant battle to make progress to the westward. As it was their winter the days were short, it being necessary to light the lamp in the binnacle in order that the man at the wheel could see the compass about three o'clock in the afternoon and keep it going until after eight the next morning. Driving a large, heavily loaded ship from 50 degrees south in the Atlantic to 50 degrees south in the Pacific is about as severe a test, both of the vessel herself and the crew she has on board, as can be found anywhere in the world. Whenever there was a chance to make any progress to the westward the ship was driven for all she would stand, because that was the only way in which we could hope to work far enough to the westward to enable us to head to the northward without going too close to the Patagonian coast.

As the mate had been taken down with a case of Cape Horn fever, it was necessary for me to stand his watch. One night after we reached the Pacific we were standing to the northward and I found myself much closer in toward land than I liked, but I felt reasonably sure I was watching the position carefully. On one of my trips to leeward, as I stood looking at the coastline, I saw the carpenter standing on the quarter. As the carpenter, cook and steward are the only men on shipboard who sleep inside all night, I was rather surprised to see him standing there and asked him why he was there. He replied that if I hadn't any objection he would like to go aft and talk to the bosun for a while. I assured him that there was no reason at all if he wanted to do so, but I thought he would be much more comfortable if he were in his bunk forward.

Leaving the carpenter, I walked over to the compass to take a bearing of the land and then walked down to leeward again and stood looking at the coastline. As I did so, the carpenter asked me if I did not think it looked pretty close. And then I knew why he was not in his bunk. I said yes, it did look close, and it was closer than I did like to have it, but I thought that we would pull away from it if the sails held; then made the remark that the ship was only 240 feet long and if we struck that point it wouldn't make any difference to him if he was in his bunk forward or aft on the quarter. His reply was that he knew that, but if we were going to strike it, he would like to be somewhere near where I was. I told him if that gave him any comfort, he was welcome to stay on the quarter as long as he liked.

Fortunately, the sails did hold and we were able to work clear of the land, and a few days afterwards had worked enough to the northward to pick up the Southeast Trades. Just as soon as we did this we knew all our difficulties were over for that voyage, for from then on into San Francisco we had no serious problems to meet, and finally arrived in San Francisco 16 October 1890, after a long passage of 157 days.

There was very little freight offering, and after the ship had been laid up for nearly a month and a half we sailed for Seattle on 5 December 1890. We had a very stormy passage, but as the prevailing wind was mostly from the southeast we made good time and arrived off Cape Flattery at night on 13 December. At that time the wind was blowing strong from the southeast, and as it was winter time the days were short in that latitude. As we rounded the cape we braced the yards sharp up on the starboard tack and headed up the straits under the main upper topsail. When I gave the order to brace the yards, the mate asked me if I was going in that night. I told him yes, I was going in and stay there as long as my nerve held out. Because of the direction of the wind we were forced to bear over toward Vancouver Island and I did not know whether or not I would want to stay in there all night, but I did know that if we decided to run out I would be able to do so unless the wind changed to the southward, and if it did I would be able to make my course up the sound.

About nine o'clock we saw the lights of a large tug coming down towards us. Unfortunately, it proved to be the British tug *Lorne* and when she found we were bound for Seattle lost all interest in us and steamed away to look for a ship that was bound for Vancouver or Nanaimo. About an hour after the *Lorne* left us we saw the lights of another tugboat. This proved to be the American tug *Tyee*. This tug was only interested in vessels bound for the American side, and when she found we were bound for Seattle she put her line aboard and started to tow us up the straits. The wind was blowing so strong that it took her over twenty hours to tow us the 100 miles we had to go from where she took hold of us. In fact, it was so stormy at the cape that three or four vessels which were closer to that point than we were when night came decided that they would stand off for the night and come in the next day. The result of their standing off, however, was that none of them got in for a week, and some were much longer getting back on the coast. This gave us a chance for good dispatch and we were able to secure a cargo and leave for San Francisco on 4 January 1891.

There was one bright side to the picture, for owing to the friends I had made on previous trips to Seattle in the *Cyrus Wakefield*, I was able to spend a very pleasant Christmas, one of the few I had been able to spend on shore since first going to sea. Our passage back to San Francisco was much longer than the upward one due to the fact that we had head winds most of the way. However, we reached port 18 January 1891, after a passage of fourteen days from Seattle.

There were still very few freight offerings; however, we finally secured a charter to load general merchandise for New York and sailed from San Francisco 1 April 1891. We had the ordinary summer weather in the North Pacific until we picked up the Northeast Trades, which carried us down nearly to the equator, where we had the usual experience of meeting with light airs, calms, and rainy weather. As the *Gibson* was not as lofty as the *Wakefield*, she did not make as good progress through these latitudes. However, we finally worked clear of the light weather and picked up the Southeast Trades which carried us down to nearly 30 degrees south latitude. After losing the trades we had variable weather until we picked up the strong westerlies of the Cape Horn region. Some of these were very heavy, but as they were mostly fair we made good progress.

I had one experience here which I think I can safely say is the only time I ever was really frightened at sea. I was standing on top of the after house

Heavy Weather to New York

while the men were checking in the main braces, when suddenly a very heavy sea came on board and washed everybody to leeward. Among the sailors was the son of one of my Seattle friends who was making the trip in order to have the experience. When the ship rolled back I could see the heads of the different men bobbing around in the water. This youngster managed to get hold of a main deck capstan, but when she gave the next roll to leeward a big six-foot black sailor we had, as he swept by to leeward, grabbed hold of the feet of the youngster who was holding onto the capstan and they both went down to leeward. My heart was in my mouth until the ship rolled to windward again and I found that this boy and all the rest of the crew were safely on board.

We had a large chicken house built on the after hatch. It was about six feet high and eight feet square, and one night when we were running before a heavy gale she shipped a sea which tore the ring bolts out of the house and it floated clear up over the rail and away to leeward without leaving a mark behind it. This will give some idea of how much water there was on the main deck when some of those heavy seas came aboard.

Trouble with the Brooklyn Bridge

In spite of the heavy weather we arrived safely in New York on 12 August 1891. As our discharging berth was above the Brooklyn Bridge, it was necessary to lower the topgallant mast in order to go under the bridge. Before leaving the vessel to arrange the docking, I instructed the mate to lower all three topgallant masts enough to give him sufficient clearance, telling him that the height of the bridge was 132 feet above high water, and to be sure that he had his masts low enough to permit us to go under it safely. After entering the ship and making the necessary arrangements for docking the vessel, I went out to her on board the tug which was to tow us into our berth. As I came alongside I looked at the masts and it seemed to me that the trucks were more than 132 feet from the water. The mate assured me, however, that I was mistaken, that there was plenty of clearance and so we started up to the dock. As we approached the bridge it did not seem to me possible for the masts to go under. The foremast did, however, but the mainmast did not, and the first thing I knew it was broken short off and the big gold ball of the main truck was coming straight down where I stood on top of the after house, so I stepped to one side to give it the right of way.

Last Time Round the Horn

We finally completed discharging our San Francisco cargo, and then, as the ship was chartered to load coal in Baltimore for San Francisco, towed to that city for loading, We sailed from Baltimore 4 November 1891. Soon after leaving Baltimore we found the main pump did not work very well, and on making a close examination found that the casting containing the valves had split. We patched this up temporarily so that it would take care of all of the water which came into the ship in the mild weather we had down to the line. I did not fancy undertaking to make the passage around Cape Horn under those conditions, so put into Rio de Janeiro 13 January 1892. I had taken the precaution to have the carpenter make a pattern of the casting which I took ashore with me at Rio, so that it was only necessary for us to be there forty-eight hours, as I knew the carpenter could put it back in place without any difficulty. This he did and we had everything in good shape long before we reached the bad weather off the Cape.

As it was summer time off the Cape, while we had more than our share of bad weather, we nevertheless had the benefit of the long days, for at that time of the year there are only two or three hours of darkness, and so it was much easier for us to handle the ship in the heavy weather we encountered. We were twenty-one days from 50 degrees south in the Atlantic to 50 degrees south in the Pacific, and from that point gradually worked our way up to the north and west until we picked up the Southeast Trades, which, of course, gave us a fair wind for crossing the equator at the desired longitude. Then came the doldrums with their light airs and calms. Once clear of these we picked up the Northeast Trades which carried us to the westward of San Francisco, but as the winds in that part of the ocean are mostly from the west, we had a fine run to port, arriving in San Francisco 1 May 1892. After the cargo was discharged, there being no business in sight, the ship was laid up at Mission Rock.

Our first visitor after the ship passed quarantine was an old friend of mine, Charlie McCarthy, who invited me to go ashore with him to breakfast. This breakfast consisted principally of coffee and ham and eggs, and although it is nearly thirty-nine years since I ate that breakfast, I still remember how good it was.

During the summer Mr. P. F. Boles, son-in-law of Mr. G. W. McNear, the largest shipper of grain out of California, and for whom I had carried several cargoes, asked me if I would be interested in entering business on shore. Owing to the fact that I had reached the highest position to be attained by anyone following the sea, there was no possible advancement for me to look forward to in continuing life on shipboard. I was thirty years old, strong, healthy, and ambitious, with no ties or responsibilities of any kind, and therefore decided to accept the offer made me by Mr. Boles. Having communicated with the owner my determination, I received instructions to turn over the command of the vessel to Captain George Wilson, which I did about 1 September 1892, thus terminating my activities as a shipmaster.

There is a vast difference in living conditions at sea between now and the days of the sailing ships, when passages might take between four and five months. The canning industry had not reached anything like its present development. There was, of course, no means of refrigeration by which you could keep fresh provisions of any kind, or secure cool water to drink. Yet, in spite of all of the severe living conditions, there was a romance and a charm about the life which is hard to describe in a way to make it attractive to anyone who has not actually lived through it; but those of us who know by personal experience just what this life was like have a very fond recollection of it. As time goes on the hardships fade away while the romance and the attractiveness of those days strengthen with the years as they pass.

A Job Ashore

Capt. Isaac Norris Hibberd (right) and his father-in-law Frederick A. Hyde, a California land owner, in an 1898 Locomobile. In possession of the author.

ISAAC NORRIS HIBBERD'S
PASSAGES ROUND CAPE HORN

Year	From	To	Ship	Capacity
1881	Philadelphia	San Francisco	*Jane Fish*	Boy
1882	San Francisco	Hull	*Jane Fish*	Boy-Seaman
1884	New York	San Francisco	*Cyrus Wakefield*	3rd Mate
1884	San Francisco	Liverpool	*Cyrus Wakefield*	1st Mate
1885	New York	San Francisco	*Cyrus Wakefield*	1st Mate
1885	San Francisco	Liverpool	*Cyrus Wakefield*	1st Mate
1886	New York	San Francisco	*Cyrus Wakefield*	1st Mate
1886	San Francisco	Dublin	*Cyrus Wakefield*	1st Mate
1887	Baltimore	San Francisco	*Cyrus Wakefield*	1st Mate
1887	San Francisco	Liverpool	*Cyrus Wakefield*	Master
1887	Liverpool	San Francisco	*Cyrus Wakefield*	Master
1888	San Francisco	Le Havre	*Cyrus Wakefield*	Master
1889	San Francisco	Liverpool	*Alexander Gibson*	Master
1890	New York	San Francisco	*Alexander Gibson*	Master
1891	San Francisco	New York	*Alexander Gibson*	Master
1891	Baltimore	San Francisco	*Alexander Gibson*	Master

Chart inside front cover: Published December, 1873
at the Hydrographic Office, Washington, D.C.,
"Cape Horn to the Magellan Strait."

Designed by Paul Gaj